In Their Hearts

Inspirational Alzheimer's Stories

Mary Margaret Britton Yearwood

Printed in Victoria, Canada

For speaking engagements, contact the author via email at
TheirHearts@aol.com

National Library of Canada Cataloguing in Publication

Yearwood, Mary Margaret Britton, 1961-
    In their hearts : inspirational Alzheimer's stories /
Mary Margaret
Britton Yearwood.
ISBN 1-55395-431-9
    I. Title.
BV4435.5.Y42 2003   259'.4196831   C2002-
905865-1

TRAFFORD

This book was published *on-demand* in cooperation with Trafford Publishing.
On-demand publishing is a unique process and service of making a book available for retail sale to the public taking advantage of on-demand manufacturing and Internet marketing. **On-demand publishing** includes promotions, retail sales, manufacturing, order fulfilment, accounting and collecting royalties on behalf of the author.

Suite 6E, 2333 Government St., Victoria, B.C. V8T 4P4, CANADA
Phone   250-383-6864   Toll-free   1-888-232-4444 (Canada & US)
Fax   250-383-6804   E-mail   sales@trafford.com
Web site   www.trafford.com   TRAFFORD PUBLISHING IS A DIVISION OF TRAFFORD HOLDINGS LTD.
Trafford Catalogue #02-1146   www.trafford.com/robots/02-1146.html

10   9   8   7   6   5   4   3

In Their Hearts

To Ward and Jane:
Follow your dreams and they'll come true.

In Their Hearts

Contents

Chapter One – Listening

Chapter Two – Smiling

Chapter Three – Going

Chapter Four – Crying

Chapter Five – Parting

Acknowledgments

During my first months as an Alzheimer's chaplain I would often run, breathless, into Woody Spackman's office with yet another amazing story at the tip of my tongue. His response to my frequent outbursts soon became, "Write it down." In the beginning it was Woody, my supervisor, who believed that I would have a multitude of opportunities to share my exciting experiences beyond his office.

I am indebted to Kathleen O'Connor, the professor who taught me to write by editing, editing, and editing some more.

Six months after I began to write about the Special Care Alzheimer's Unit, I intersected, via e-mail, with a writer in Massachusetts. Harvey Blume had begun a quest to know the unknowable. In my case, his cyber-journey had led him to a high-functioning autistic who had been slow to acquire language skills in her childhood. Just as I saw the heart and intellect of persons with Alzheimer's disease, Harvey saw the heart and intellect in me. He was not fooled by my small vocabulary. He knew I had a lot more to offer to the world than most people thought. Harvey's ongoing enthusiastic affirmations helped me to create most of the words in this book.

In Their Hearts

My first audience, besides Woody, Harvey and my family, was my fellow chaplains. Their professional feedback was critical to my self-esteem as a minister of persons with Alzheimer's disease.

Walker Knight was the first to publish one of my stories, and it made a world of difference in my writing to feel as if my audience had grown.

Five excellent readers helped to eliminate the grammatical errors in my manuscript. These readers were Janet Lutz, Jackie Smythe, Julia House, Kay Keels, and my cousin James Moore. Janet, a chaplain supervisor, also provided bimonthly encouragement and refreshing, positive energy that helped me endure the many necessary grammatical edits.

My sister, Elizabeth Ellis, who is a missionary and teacher of English in Japan, prayed with some of her students for the success of this book long before it was a book.

A few years ago I gave some of my stories to Don Saliers, one of my seminary professors. He suggested I keep writing when I barely understood how much work was involved in publishing. Wayne Ewing, author of <u>Tears in God's Bottle: Reflections on Alzheimer's Giving</u>, shared his wisdom about the road to publishing and made me feel less lonely on my own path. His poetic e-mails were always happily received. Ginny Helms, with our local Alzheimer's chapter, pointed me to many of my speaking engagements. She also took me to several lunches when I felt as if I would never finish the book. Her words and good food were a welcome cure for the doldrums.

Through the entire process my loving therapist, Chris Lahowitch, has kept me smiling and laughing despite my protests to remain a serious soul. Chris has always been able to see the good in my life before I was able to admit to it.

My son, Ward, has continuously prodded me to hurry up and get rich from my writing. He also helped to create the title of this volume. My daughter, Jane, has kept me grounded by insisting each day that I finish editing my stories and get off the computer so that she can check her e-mail or talk on the phone. And Mary Crist Brown, who lives with me, has loved me day in and day out. Mary Crist is a good soul and I am fortunate to know her.

Thank you, all!

In Their Hearts

Foreword

by Harvey Blume

My friendship with Mary Margaret Britton Yearwood ("MM" as I came to know her) began in cyberspace. I was doing research on autism; she was an active member of an Internet forum (or listserv) called Independent Living (InLv), run by and for the most part for high-functioning autistics (HFAs). Encountering InLv, I felt a bit like a forest traveler who comes unexpectedly upon a clearing filled with huts and human activity. I had, in fact, stumbled into a cyber-tribe of autistics. Of course, there wasn't supposed to be any such thing: autistics were supposed to be solitary and incommunicative. InLv gave the lie to that; e-mail allowed a community of high-functioning autistics to coalesce and flourish.

But what were the rules and customs of this community--especially in relation to an outsider like me? As I found almost immediately, outsiders like me belonged, according to local lore, to a very different tribe, that of NTs, or neuro-typicals. NTs defined the neurological norm in our society, blithely assuming that the way our minds worked was the only valid way, and all else was pathological. One reason HFAs had gathered online was to relieve themselves of the need to pass--to try to act like NTs--in an NT world. Still, with my eagerness to learn about autism and other neurological differences, I was welcomed. So far as autism was concerned, I was made to feel like a fellow traveler.

This was in no small measure due to my having found, in MM, an excellent guide to the ways of autism. She showed me how HFA perceptions of the world differed from NT perceptions, explaining, for example, that touch can be painful for autistics, and the lack of it painful as well:

> I think that we were not able to be held
> as children because of this weird skin
> we have.
> No mama held me to make it better.
> No daddy said it would be all right.
> This forced us to hold ourselves
> when the monsters came at night.
> We held ourselves together
> to keep from breaking apart,
> to keep from getting lost
> in that great void that awaits all autistics.
> Because we had to do this on our own,
> we used so much more energy
> than others just to exist
> in this world.
> And then we exhaust ourselves.

In Their Hearts

Often, MM sent me autobiographical writings; at other times we exchanged commentary on aspects of American culture shared by HFAs and NTs alike. Here, for example, is a short piece by MM about the meaning of one of our favorite shared texts, Star Trek (Data, if he needs any introduction, is Star Trek's android):

My absolute favorite Star Trek
with Data
was the time he had made contact
with a more primitive race
and Picard told him
to cut it off immediately
but first Data
wanted Picard and the
rest of the officers
to hear the most recent transmission
and totally out of the blue
we hear a girl's voice
say into the airwaves,
"Data, Data, are you there?
Data where are you? I am scared."
And all of a sudden
the prime directive wasn't so clear
to anyone.
Data forces the hand of the humans
by having even more compassion.

In Their Hearts

He points to the paradoxes
of their culture.

And here is MM writing about Hikari Oe, a
composer of music who was born with neurological
damage. She says his music is

like a hand rests on my heart
and tells me everything will be well with my soul,
like the rhythm slows
down my anxious autistic heart
to the rhythm it should be if a mama was there
to hold me,
like Hikari understands
that autistics need to know what it is like
to be held by their mother and daddy,
and so he is able to share that heldness
that I have so little of in my life,
I feel complete when I hear it,
like I don't have to struggle and bang my head,
maybe this is autistic heaven,
that he has made for me.
The differently wired brain
is just fine for a little while.

As is obvious, MM has a distinct and vigorous
writing style. She works with short lines not because

In Their Hearts

they look like poetry but because they spare her the headaches long lines of text can give her. I got to know her well through her short-lined emails, as she got to know me through my more conventional-looking posts. And get to know me she did. MM was not content to be observed, studied, learned from. Her empathy, curiosity, and intelligence were too untrammeled for that. If I was going to study autism, she was going to ask me why I cared to do so, what I had to gain from it, and what it taught me about myself. ("What makes you want to know us?" she asked me. "Are you, too, hidden in your own way?") Often I felt whatever lens I was using to observe MM got turned around somewhere in the process so that it pointed right back at me. Getting to know MM, in other words, was inseparable from getting to know myself.

When MM began work with Alzheimer's patients, it seemed that in a sense, she had come home. The terrible reductions brought about by Alzheimer's can make sufferers seem opaque, remote, and in-communicative. For MM, however, one part of what has been subtracted from Alzheimer's sufferers is their capacity to comprehend social conventions that she, too, as a high-functioning autistic, finds well nigh indecipherable. In MM's eyes, Alzheimer's boils people down to essences. They lose their talents for evasion and self-evasion. They become starkly visible. When

she deals with them, there are no masks or niceties--
only truths.

MM's profiles of Alzheimer's remind me of the
late work of the great painter Willem de Kooning. De
Kooning's work had always been known for its overflow
of paint and energy--women who were as abundant as
landscapes, landscapes that looked like women. Then,
in his later years, de Kooning contracted Alzheimer's
disease. He did not cease to paint, but the paintings
changed. They became radically simplified. There was
far more room for white space and for absence. All the
action was concentrated into long, colorful, flowing
lines. Some critics derided the late painting, warning
viewers not to mistake these sad symptoms of
declining skill for anything like real art. To me, however,
these paintings seemed superb in their own right. What
had changed was not so much the degree of skill as
the neurological context. De Kooning was as great a
painter of Alzheimer's as he had once been of
landscapes and women. What remained alive for him,
even after Alzheimer's had done its damage, was the
love of form, color, and paint itself.

This simplified, concentrated flow of energy and
personality is what MM captures in her profiles of
Alzheimer's patients.

I need to say something about the language MM
uses in the following pages. It is replete with Christian

In Their Hearts

imagery. As MM tells it, Jesus keeps an eye on the Alzheimer's ward, sometimes even materializing as a patient. Usually, I am immune to such characterizations. I count myself as increasingly, even defiantly, secular. Yet, to my surprise--and MM's--I found myself enjoying and being moved by these stories. I realized that what matters is not whether the language is religious or secular but how truly it is spoken. MM is never straining for effects in these tales. She is reflecting on loss and suffering, on continuity and identity. Jesus appears in these reflections not as a grand and majestic presence but as a fellow sufferer. The patients on the Alzheimer's ward don't have to go out of their way to meet him. He might be someone in an adjacent room, or on another floor, or one whose bed has suddenly, sadly, become empty overnight.

Harvey is a freelance writer in Cambridge, Mass., who has written frequently on neurology and on the arts.

In Their Hearts

Introduction

In 1966 my Aunt Jane met me for the first time at my fifth birthday party. My family lived in an apartment just outside of Washington, D.C., where my father worked at the Pentagon as a computer programmer. My mother, an elementary school teacher, had invited some of the neighborhood children to my party. When Aunt Jane arrived, there were children dashing about our home but none of those children was the niece that she sought. After looking through most of the apartment, my aunt asked my mother the whereabouts of the birthday girl. My mother pointed to the dining room table decorated with a birthday tablecloth. Aunt Jane walked over to the table and lifted the cloth. Under the table she found a little girl with big brown eyes.

My aunt said matter-of-factly, "Hello, Mary Margaret. I am your Aunt Jane. You don't have to come out from under the table for me. You can enjoy the party in your own way. I just wanted to introduce myself." Aunt Jane let go of the tablecloth and the child under the table was alone again.

Thirty more years passed before I understood why I avoid crowds. I discovered that my five senses have been extra sensitive since birth. It feels as if the world is screaming in my ears, blinding my eyes, and pinching my skin. Normal conversations give me a headache after five minutes and hugs almost always feel like torture. My mother's good intentions to coax me out of my shell by surrounding me with playmates might have been successful if I had feared people instead of people sounds. As a child I wasn't emotionally shy. I was sensory overloaded. My symptoms fit a neurological condition called Asperger's Syndrome. Asperger's is a high-functioning branch of autism. As an adult I am fortunate to receive emotional support and education about my neurological differences from the Emory Autism Research Center and from other persons with Asperger's Syndrome whom I have met through special e-mail lists.

However, in 1966 neither my parents nor my doctors were able to explain my peculiar behavior. Words like "stubborn," "spoiled," and "emotionally immature" would be attached to me throughout my life. Unable to defend my actions, I carried the weight of these dehumanizing words until 1995, the year I learned the new words "Asperger's Syndrome" and "high-functioning autism." Although I consider myself lucky to have found healing information after all those years, I know in my heart I am never very far from that little girl under the table.

Language development can be difficult for some persons on the autistic spectrum. For me English is like

In Their Hearts

a second language even though I was raised in an English-speaking household. My first language is not verbal; it is a constant series of pictures I see in my mind's eye. Usually these pictures are called the imagination. In my case the very vivid pictures of the imagination appear more real to me than the world outside my body. As a child my internal world of complex pictures called me away from the land of words in which most humans live; consequently my ability to speak was delayed. Even now I continually see pictures flashing in my mind's eye, whether I am awake or asleep. I have very elaborate daydreams and night dreams. I do not have a way to turn off the graphic movies of my internal theatre. As an adult my turned-on-high senses continue to make it difficult for me to be in crowds. The fascinating pictures in my mind's eye still call me away from life outside of myself. My favorite places continue to be quiet corners away from the boisterous activities of humanity. In a quiet space I am free to be my favorite self surrounded by my internal images of greater and better things.

When I was a teenager, my father coached my siblings and me how to enter into intellectual conversations about the theatrical performances he so loved. This informal training finally gave me, the child who said so little, a way to converse with the rest of humanity. My father had become a part-time professional actor in Atlanta and his excitement for his work spilled over to the rest of the family. At least once a month my older brother, younger sister, and I were coached to give feedback on the plays that my father and his friends passionately performed. We were expected to pick out and defend themes and to analyze the characters. If we did not think an actor fit his or her role, my father opened the conversation to include our young voices. Did we find the incongruity to be the fault of the director, actor, writer, or any combination of the three? Gradually my siblings and I learned to express our opinions about the live performances we were privileged to watch from the first rehearsals to the final productions. This was not a dry, dead process. It was an exciting and electric awakening of our teenage souls. I am very thankful that my father gave me the tools to enter important, philosophic discussions that have the potential to turn into questions and discussions about my own life. I think that is where my father was driving us: he wanted us to be self-reflective.

At the age of seventeen, I entered Georgia Tech as a math major. Analytic problem-solving had become a constant part of the pictures in my head. While at Tech, I began to draw mathematical models of God. For example, perhaps God is like a point in the center of a clear sphere. Humanity is scattered on the outside

In Their Hearts

of the sphere, just as we are scattered around this orb we call Earth. In my math model there is no possible way to get physically closer to God but there is a way to see other sides of God. To better understand God, one needs to get to know the people from different sections of the clear sphere. The different sections on the sphere can represent actual land masses on our planet or different philosophies of life, or both. This was just one picture that came into my head in the middle of doing my calculus homework. Unfortunately, I did not have the ability to turn off the math movies in my mind's eye, and they haunted me into the wee hours of the morning.

Between the too-many-problem-solving pictures in my head and the over-populated classrooms that were common at Georgia Tech in the early 1980s, I began to attend classes less and less. Also, because of sports injuries, I became locked into a series of major knee surgeries. The long recoveries from the surgeries pulled me away from the fast pace of an institution like Georgia Institute of Technology. I was like a ship drifting from its dock. Because of my ongoing neurological and physical problems, I became passionate about finding the face of God. I desperately wanted to know why I seemed destined forever to be cut off from other humans. Since I was a Baptist like my mother, I prayed to Jesus when I felt overwhelmed with

In Their Hearts

loneliness. I also became both a philosophy and a religion major at a small local college that had tiny classes.

At my new school I was able to hear and read about major philosophers I had not studied before. I soon fell in love with matching my analytic mind to Plato, Aristotle, Aquinas, and Kierkegaard. My debates with the major philosophers' writings and also with my philosophy professor, Deal Hudson, were some of the happiest moments of my young adulthood. The voice my father had coaxed out of its shell was beginning to mature.

Unfortunately my happiness was abruptly interrupted by the death of one of my closest friends from childhood. For different reasons, we had both ended up at the same small college. As children and teenagers we had been peers on the softball field and basketball court. At the age of twenty-one we were learning to discuss the important issues of our lives on our drive to class each morning. On the day I was to present a major philosophy project, my friend dropped me off in front of the college and said, "It's going to be a great day!" Fifteen minutes later she had a fatal car crash.

This event impacted my life in at least two major ways. First, instead of continuing to boldly explore my academic career, I ran to the imagined safety of marriage and motherhood. Second, for the first time, I understood the power of the English language. I wanted to tell somebody, anybody, about my friend of fourteen years whose life and death had dramatically touched me. I desperately wanted to reach beyond my world of one. Not knowing how to ask any human for a forum in which to speak, I earnestly prayed to Jesus. "Please, please, let me say something! I can't handle this in silence." Perhaps I didn't know what I was asking, but the answer to that prayer changed my life forever. Minutes before our college's weekly chapel service (four days after the accident) I was asked to say something about my childhood buddy in front of the other students and my professors. I was ready. In that moment, all those years of unspoken feelings came to the surface in the form of a beautiful eulogy. After the service the dean of the school said I was one of the finest preachers she had ever heard. I said, "I know," accepting my charismatic voice as a fact. The child who rarely spoke was now a gifted public speaker. I had preached my first sermon, but I would spend years hiding away in my new-found family life before I took my preaching career seriously.

By the time my children were ages one and two, I was dreaming about my return to the academic arena. Again I prayed, this time to go to seminary. In seminary I learned about Bible research and preaching techniques from Gail O'Day. My studies helped me realize that I was young and naïve in thought. What good was a charismatic voice without wisdom?

Because it forces students to discover why they believe what they believe, seminary has a way of exposing weaknesses in the lives of its students. My second year of seminary uncovered the problems in my marriage and became the year of my divorce. This time I sought refuge from my pain behind the doors of therapy and the theological classroom. The many difficulties that come with a divorce made me feel as if I were moving backwards from becoming a wise preacher. Twelve years after the fact, I know the divorce helped to move me from an arrogant view of life to a humbler, wiser place. At the time, I decided I should stay in school. It brought some order to my chaos by giving me new language to describe my life situation. I studied modern liberation movements with Rebecca Chopp. Some of the liberationists compared their movements to the liberation of the Israelites by Moses that I was encountering in my Hebrew Bible courses.

After I received my Master of Divinity from Candler School of Theology at Emory University in 1992, I pursued a Master of Theology in Old Testament (Hebrew Bible) at Columbia Theological Seminary in Decatur, Georgia. My goal was to become a Hebrew

In Their Hearts

Bible professor. While at Columbia Seminary, I became interested in an area of expertise called Rhetorical Criticism. Rhetorical Criticism finds meaning in the stories and speeches in scripture by examining Hebrew words in detail. As a student I was taught to find recurring phrases and sentence structures to help map recurring Bible themes.[1] It was a natural progression for me to study Rhetorical Criticism because I already read scripture as if I were watching my father's plays.

My rhetorical studies led me to notice the stark contrast between those characters that speak in the scriptures and those characters that do not speak. I also began to wonder why some of the characters in these faith stories used certain phrases more than others. I pondered how the repeated phrases, or even repeated silence, helped develop characters and major themes. I struggled to understand my own humanity as a woman who had spent a lifetime saying so little to humans but had an internal dialogue in my picture-language with Jesus. The more I studied the scriptures, the more I was drawn to female metaphors of Israel, particularly the ones where "she" did not speak "her" mind. (Hosea 2) What kept the Israelites from speaking

---

[1]For more information on the topic, Pyllis Trible has written a book called Rhetorical Criticism: Context Method, and the Book of Jonah (Minneapolis: Fortress Press, 1994).

In Their Hearts

up? I wondered. How different was I as a woman with Asperger's Syndrome in modern days?

In the Hebrew scriptures humans are not the only players on the stage. God is included in the Israelites' daily drama and considered a character in the ancient stories. This is similar to the theology that my maternal grandmother, Ola Parker Moore, left to her children and grandchildren. She thought Jesus, the incarnation of God, took an active part in her life. My mother remembers my grandmother telling her about the day Jesus appeared in a vision to the young Ola on her journey from her home in North Carolina to teach in the Kentucky mountains. According to my grandmother, Jesus let her know that he would never forsake her because she, Ola, was on this earth to do God's work. In my grandmother's later years "God's work" included teaching the adult Sunday School class at Bethlehem Baptist Church in North Carolina, cooking and sewing for her six children, educating the community on how to take care of themselves with the help of the county extension service, and giving aid to persons less fortunate than herself. Ola Parker Moore believed that keeping busy by doing God's work kept a person out of mischief. Although my own theology continues to grow more each day, I have never let go of my grandmother's belief that Jesus is a part of my daily life as God was a part of the Israelites' daily lives.

In Their Hearts

I also continue to carry on the tradition of filling my day with God's work to keep out of mischief, although I do like a bit of fun here and there.

As I began to apply to seminaries for a Ph.D. in Hebrew Bible, professors in different parts of the country told me Hebrew teaching positions were rare. I also encountered difficulties making a high enough vocabulary score on the Graduate Record Exam because of my Asperger's Syndrome. Scoring well on the GRE was a requirement for most graduate programs. After much prayer I decided to try hospital chaplaincy until more professors retired and I had built up my English vocabulary. Ironically, I could read Hebrew, Aramaic, Greek and German, but my English could never quite catch up to academia's standards.

I asked to be a chaplain in the emergency room because many societal expectations are dropped during times of trauma. As I am a person with Asperger's Syndrome who has difficulty with the usual daily social norms, the emergency room feels "at home" to me. However, I was not assigned to the emergency room. I was given the Alzheimer's Special Care Unit and that is where I found my "neurological cousins."

Alzheimer's disease is one of many types of dementia. A person can experience dementia because of multiple strokes, infections, depression, drug abuse, alcoholism, heart attacks and many other reasons. Some forms of dementia are reversible. Alzheimer's disease is an irreversible, gradually progressive dementia. There is no cure for the disease at this time. Sadly, Alzheimer's is eventually fatal.[2]

I immediately found that individuals with Asperger's Syndrome and Alzheimer's disease have a lot in common. Like myself, persons with Alzheimer's often get lost in their own world, make little eye contact, have a small vocabulary, don't recognize the person in the mirror, and don't always see the difference between animate creatures and inanimate objects. I couldn't believe it at first: I had found a population of people who were slipping under the table of life and were experiencing the party in their own way.

As the chaplain on the dementia unit, I entered a real life drama that would fill my heart more than any stage play or Bible story. Being my grandmother's spiritual heir, I saw visions of Jesus on the Alzheimer's unit. In my eyes Jesus was very much a part of my work. Jesus both lived in the residents and served them as their Good Shepherd (Psalm 23, John 10). But

[2]Carolyn French, Eve Levine, and Nancy Morrison, Understanding and Caring for the Person with Alzheimer's Disease: A Practical Guide Prepared by the Atlanta Area Chapter Alzheimer's Association (Atlanta: Atlanta Area Chapter Alzheimer's Association, Inc., 1996), 4-7.

In Their Hearts

my own spirituality is not limited to Biblical metaphors and neither was the spirituality of my residents. Together we would discover many important and complex life themes, still very much alive despite the dementia. While other professionals were recording cognitive losses, I was discovering a gold mine of spirituality still intact in persons with Alzheimer's disease. I began to speak in public arenas about my experiences as a chaplain on the Special Care Alzheimer's unit where I found myself singing a theme song to match what I was witnessing every day. It went like this: "Though cognition is lost, spirituality remains. Whatever lives in your heart of hearts, your soul of souls, never goes away. Alzheimer's may steal your brain cells but it can't steal your soul. Who you are and what you believe never leaves." I had finally found the wisdom I had been seeking to match my charismatic voice.

Five years ago I arrived at The Special Care Alzheimer's Unit with my prejudices and my ignorance about the aging population. In the Hebrew Bible the word "ruah" means spirit, wind, and breath.[3] It was the "ruah" of the Special Care Alzheimer's Unit that tapped

---

[3]Francis Brown, S.R. Driver, and Charles A. Briggs, <u>The New Brown – Driver – Briggs – Gesenius Hebrew and English Lexicon</u> (Peabody: Massachusetts: Hendrickson Publishers, 1979), 924-926.

In Their Hearts

me on the shoulder and asked me to dance with the residents that lived and died there. This is the record of my sacred time in and with the spirit, wind, and breath of an Alzheimer's unit in Atlanta from August 1997 to August 1999.

Mary Margaret
December 2002

Chapter One - Listening

Listening

Persons with Alzheimer's disease are just as diverse in personality as the rest of society. Dementia robs individuals of their communication skills and their ability to remember the details of certain events. These deficits do not make persons with Alzheimer's disease any less human. They still have individual histories, thoughts, and desires. I try to take each person seriously as an adult who knows his or her individual mind, no matter how much verbal communication is absent and no matter how much memory is lost.

Do You Know My Name?
Do You Know Me?

"My name is Julia Norman,[4] N-o-r-m-a-n. Ya' got that?" Those were the first words from the first person to greet me on my first day as the chaplain on the Alzheimer's Special Care Unit. Julia Norman didn't wait for an answer. Instead, she continued, "You're new around here." She spoke in a "take charge" tone of voice as she grabbed my hand. Apparently she had a right to all persons who crossed over into her territory. I had not offered my hand, but she took it nonetheless.

"Yes, ma'am," I finally muttered to the all-knowing Julia Norman, who was leading me to God-only-knew-where. I cleared my throat to muster some authority, for Julia spoke with years of being on top of things and I was not quite ready to submit to her will. This was not how I had planned to begin my chaplaincy and I would make that clear as soon as I could get into the conversation. I said in my most professional voice to the woman who had kidnapped my body via my hand, "I am Mary Margaret, the new chaplain around here."

---

[4]All the names of Alzheimer's patients and their families have been changed. The names of staff who work with Alzheimer's patients also have been changed.

Julia Norman patted my hand as she would a child. "Well, that's just fine, dear. I've always said, 'We need more good folks in this here world.' And you look like good folk to me."

I grimaced as I felt a layer of shyness blanket my being. But Julia Norman didn't seem to notice. She had more to say, which meant my quiet suited her just fine.

"Well, darling, come with me. My room is right down here as you can see and everyone likes to sit in that big room over there. My name is Julia Norman. N-o-r-m-a-n. You got that?"

"Uh, yes, ma'am, Julia Norman, N-o-r-m-a-n."

"Good girl! Let's sit on this here bench. I'm pooped. Whew."

I had no choice but to sit down too. Julia Norman, N-o-r-m-a-n, still had my hand and so I sat down and considered my limited options. I looked around the unit from my new locale and no one, neither resident nor worker, looked back at me. In many ways it was just Julia Norman and me alone on that bench in a strange new land.

"Do you know anything about the Normans?" my bench-mate continued. "We're right-smart hard-working people, you know. Been in these parts for some time. I was going to be a teacher a long time ago. But Mama was so sick. I had to stay home and take care of the other children. There were eleven us, you know, and I was the oldest girl. Mama would be feeling poorly and people would ask her to do things and she would say, 'Julia can do it.' And I did. 'Cause Mama always could rely on me."

"I bet she could."

For a moment I thought Julia Norman was going to fall asleep because she closed her eyes and became quiet for the first time since I had stepped off the elevator. But in no time she was up again walking me up and down the hall.

"My name's Julia Norman. N-o-r-m-a-n. Ya' got that?" she said yet again as if there would be test on it the next day.

"Yes, ma'am," I responded with ears that wanted to hear.

"You ever heard of the Normans? Mama always said we were a right-smart hard-working bunch. I do believe she was right. Now Billy--he's my son--he's a whippersnapper, that one. Lord, that boy is bright and he puts his whole heart into his work. I was going to be a teacher, ya' know. And I did teach for a year or two. But between taking care of my sisters and brothers and then I had my own family--well, I really didn't ever get to teach as much as I wanted. Oh boy, I did love teaching!"

I suppose at any other time I would have let Julia's repetitious words go in one ear and out the other. And I probably would have pointed to her dementia. But my supervisor, Woody Spackman,[5] had just taught my colleagues and me that pastoral care to the elderly included a look at the worth of one's life.[6] With my undergraduate degree in philosophy, I interpreted Woody's didactic to mean our aging population is asking questions such as: "Did I do anything that will make you remember me? Did I finish my mission here on this earth? My life didn't turn out the way I dreamed it and now it is coming to an end. How do I live and die with the knowledge that I didn't get to everything I wanted to accomplish?" And so I decided to interpret Julia Norman's repeated attempts to tell me about her life as more than dementia. I decided to pay attention to *what* she was repeating. She was repeating the importance of a good name in a good family vs. her individual desire to make her own name separate from her loved ones. The longer I remained on the Special Care Alzheimer's Unit, the more I was of the opinion that Julia Norman, N-o-r-m-a-n, and others like her were not exempt from spiritual

---

[5] His name is not changed.

[6] Woody Spackman's didactic included Erik Erikson's psychosocial crises, the last of which is "Despair vs. Integrity" in the elder years.

needs. In particular, Julia Norman wanted me to know all that hard work she did for her sick "mama" had kept her from living the life she had dreamed. But as a Norman she had no other choice but to have lived the life she did.

"Do you know my name? Do you know me? Listen, chaplain, and I will tell you about my life in these stories I recite again and again. I worked hard and I loved hard but most of my dreams never came true. And now I am an old woman and I am trusting you not to push me away with your platitudes. Tell me. Tell me. Did my life have worth in your eyes and God's eyes, too?"

Before I left that first day on the unit, Julia Norman told me at least five more times how to spell her name. In between the spelling lessons she continued to tell me her life story so precious and so true.

"Do you know my name? Do you know me? Julia Norman. N-o-r-m-a-n."

When the Mute Speak

By my third month as a chaplain I had seen a number of bizarre events that can be seen only on an Alzheimer's Unit. I had seen a woman stand right in front of her room and ask where she lived. I had been screamed at, swung at, pinched and pushed. I had seen people who had just eaten claim they were being starved to death. The more I experienced these Alzheimer's moments, the more I became a smug veteran of the unit. I honestly thought there weren't many more surprises for me. Etched in my memory was the first time I led a devotional service on the Alzheimer's unit and I naively asked for prayer requests. No one said a word. Not a single utterance came from the lips of the residents, which was unusual in itself. I stood in that awkward moment and promised myself I would never fall into that trap again. Lesson number umpteen: Don't ask persons with dementia for prayer requests. From then on I stepped back and let Melanie, the activity therapist, play familiar hymns and I delivered my short homilies in story form. Most of the residents showed signs that they understood what I was saying by nodding their heads in recognition or by chiming in with appropriate statements and questions.

Slowly I became used to the familiar rhythm of the Monday afternoon devotional service on Annie's floor. Annie was one of the passive participants during worship. She had become almost entirely nonverbal. Annie's vocabulary had been reduced to answering questions with a "yes" or "no." She also was able to say her daughter's name and occasionally she mumbled a couple of words that only she understood. But mostly Annie said nothing at all. The disease process seemed to have robbed her of her native tongue.

Staying with the lectionary reading one winter afternoon, my five-minute meditation was about Hannah praying what I called a "selfish" prayer. Hannah had prayed that God would give her a son. (I Samuel 1:10-13) She prayed for herself in the house of the Lord, not for somebody else. As a Baptist, I had been taught to pray for missionaries around the world and also for those persons less fortunate than myself. It had never been said out loud, but my childhood's church's stress on missionaries and the outcast made me think it was selfish to pray for myself. I found it odd that Hannah was not ashamed to pray for herself. Even more unusual was the fact that God gave Hannah the desire of her heart. (I Samuel 1:10) Not only did she get a son, but her son, Samuel, became one of the most powerful people in Israel. After I expressed my feelings about Hannah's prayer to the dementia residents, I suggested that we on the unit be like Hannah and pray for ourselves. If Hannah could pray for herself with such positive results, certainly we could do the same.

I walked up to each resident and asked if I could pray for him or her. Almost everyone in the room gave an affirmative response. I respected the few who didn't respond by leaving them alone. Many of the residents like Annie said "yes" to prayer but could not tell me exactly what they wanted. So I held their hands and prayed that God would give them the desires of their hearts and would be with them in mind, body and soul.

When I finally finished praying for the residents, Melanie, the activity therapist, said, "What about me? Are you going to pray for me?" Her request made me stop for a moment. Ministering to persons with Alzheimer's disease comes naturally to me because just as they have neurological differences, I too have some neurological differences with my Asperger's Syndrome.[7] I would have to switch gears to pray for Melanie. To buy a little transition time I blurted out, "Who is going to pray for Melanie?" I didn't really expect an answer.

Up jumped Deborah, a dementia resident whose individual words were somewhat clear but groups of words were almost always scrambled. Deborah walked

---

[7]Asperger's is a high-functioning form of autism. My neurological differences are explained in more detail in the Introduction.

over to Melanie and placed her hands on Melanie's head. Then Deborah did an amazing thing: she prayed. She prayed clearly so that we could all understand her. Her words were not scrambled. Deborah prayed that Melanie would know that God would love her wherever Melanie went in this world. Both Melanie and I were in shock. Not only were we having a hard time believing Deborah's words were unscrambled, but Melanie had told me in private that she and her husband sometimes considered being missionaries to another part of the world.

In her excitement over Deborah's prayer, Melanie asked who was going to pray for me. No one answered in words, but Annie, sitting right in front of me, looked at me with her eyes shining in anticipation. I said, "Annie, do you want to pray for me?"

Annie shook her head in an affirmative nod as she said, "Yes." I took her by the hand until she was standing in front of my chair. I sat down and Annie automatically put her hands on my head.

"What are you going to pray, Annie?" I asked. This time I truly did not expect an answer because Annie was further along in her verbal decline than Deborah.

But Annie had an answer. She opened her mouth and said, "I'm going to pray that you know that God loves you very, very much and holds you close." I blinked at her in shock. My autistic skin has kept me from being held most of my life and the thought of God holding me close was beyond my comprehension. I waited to see if Annie was going to say more.

When she didn't, I exclaimed, "Oh, Annie! You spoke!"

Annie said, "Yes, I spoke. I prayed!"

I stood up and Annie and I danced around the room as I announced over and over again, "Annie prayed! Annie prayed! Annie prayed for me!"

Annie's eyes continued to glow as she said over and over, "I prayed!"

Melanie ran out to the nurses' station and said, "People who haven't spoken in months are praying in here!" I'm sure the nursing staff thought she was going crazy.

After that amazing day of prayer, Annie always recognized me. She would grab my hand as soon as she spied me on the unit and her eyes would sparkle as she related to me all kinds of details only she understood. Deborah continued to walk to the front of the room during the devotional service each week. She would take my hand, bow her head, and pray her scrambled prayers.

I don't know if Deborah or Annie will ever pray as clearly as they did on that special day. But who am I to limit Deborah, Annie, and God?

(Postscript: Two years later I became discour-
aged by the long process of writing and trying to
publish a book. I was at my lowest point. I thought
about hiding my manuscript and never looking at it
again. That very same day my son, Ward, asked to
visit a new friend. Sensing my uneasiness about
another new association, Wardy said, "Paul's[8] dad is a
minister like you. He pastors a Methodist church near
here." A few minutes later Paul's mother called me and
asked where I worked. When I told her, she related to
me that Paul's grandmother was the woman I called
Deborah. I laughed at such a coincidence in a big city
and then I picked up my manuscript and started writing
again.)

---

[8]Paul's name is used by permission of his mother.

To Be Free

She had a bungalow with an attic that looked out over the hills. Bohemian art students from far and wide sketched and painted and learned to love life in that attic of hers. She herself was a great painter. Her parents must have known she would be someone important, for they named her Victoria--a grand name for an artist.

Now she has forgotten how to pick up her paint brush that is right in front of her. She can't even sketch with the stick we call a pencil. Some days she doesn't even remember that she is the one who composed the paintings that crowd her tiny bedroom's walls.

"I want to go home!" she wails like a lone child in a vast forest. "Please, I must get back to my attic. I miss it so." Her voice quivers with fear and I feel her quivering go inside of me. *Is this my destiny? Is this who I am to be?*

All our visits are lonely, painful. Should I even come? What does the cry of one lone woman mean when so many others need me?

I am invited to join a cooking class taught by one of the city's great chefs. We are making cupcakes. While others eat their simple creations, Victoria is still decorating her piece of art.

"Oh my god!" I think to myself. How beautiful! How could one cupcake be so much? "How did you do that, Victoria?"

So intent is she on her masterpiece, she doesn't look up to respond to me. But she smiles a rare smile at her beautiful cupcake and sighs, "Isn't it wonderful to be free!"

To be free! Jesus came to set the captives free. Victoria lived that philosophy of liberty in her attic long ago. Today one tiny cupcake helps her recapture the freedom of her soul.

"Make cupcakes every day," I say to the rest of the staff in the careplan the next week.

"What?" They are perplexed by such odd advice.

I explain how much Victoria enjoyed decorating her cupcake. I conclude my little monologue with "Make cupcakes every day. Victoria will be happy and we will be free from her daily agony."

"Are you crazy? We don't have the staff for that."

Maybe I am a little crazy, for inside of me lies a belief that the cry of one lone woman is somehow connected to setting us all free. Connected to you and me. If I don't listen to her, who will listen to me? Who will listen to me?

Fire Drill

He stands at the door of our weekly devotion, one foot in, one foot out. He reminds me of a very tall egret towering over us. Crowds aren't his thing, never were, never will be. Please, please don't touch him. His shy ways won't allow it.

"Would you like to join us, Mr. Jackson?" I ask and he takes one step back.

"Oh no, thank you. You go ahead, I'll just stand right here if that is okay," he stutters politely.

"Okay, Mr. Jackson, but you are welcome to join us any time."

Some days he insists a taxi will take him home. "It is just down the street, 72 Mockingbird Lane."

But I know home is 500 miles away at least, and it would be a pretty expensive taxi ride.

When my reality does not match his, he sees me as the enemy. "Why won't you let me go home?" he barks.

I try to explain to him, "Your son has paid for a room for you to stay here tonight."

"What has he got to do with this, for Pete's sake?" Mr. Jackson's nice manners have more than disappeared. "Just let me call a taxi and I can be on my way!"

Oh, Mr. Jackson, no taxi is coming today or next week. We are stuck with each other. Can't you see?

Most days he doesn't tell me much about himself, although he can talk just fine. He says I can come and sit with him if I sit quietly in his room.

"It's cold in here. Can you turn up the heat?" his soft voice tickles the silence.

I am burning up as usual as I look at his emaciated arms. "Here, let me get you a sweater, Mr. Jackson."

"I appreciate that. Thank you."

On a Thursday in the middle of January we have a fire drill. The site of the pretend fire is the VERY MIDDLE of the Alzheimer's unit! There is a bright red strobe light turning with a siren roaring in our ears. Residents are screaming, caretakers are racing, hearts are beating wildly!

"COME WITH ME!!" we yell over it all, doing our best to get everyone behind the fire door. Some residents want to touch the scarlet strobe light. Others walk in the opposite direction. Caretakers are exhausted before we are even started. Mr. Jackson stands frozen like a statue in front of a courthouse, hands over his ears.

"Mr. Jackson, come with me!" I scream above the roar as I reach behind his elbow, not remembering his code against touch.

"NO! LET GO!" he shouts as he pulls away from me.

"Mr. Jackson, I need you to go behind that fire door!" I yell.

"Why didn't you say so!" he yells back to me. "You didn't have to grab me!" His feet are still glued to the floor.

I, on the other hand, am becoming more unglued by the moment. O Lord, why should I even try? Why can't I just run and hide? I know Mr. Jackson is one of your children. It sure would help if you would move him, because I sure can't.

Mr. Jackson's long poking finger jabs into my shoulder. "Where did you say I need to go to get away from this commotion?"

"Behind that door. I won't grab you any more. Just follow the crowd."

Caretakers are pulling residents two at a time as quickly as old feet will move. But Mr. Jackson and I are still inches from the bright light.

"Why aren't you moving, Mr. Jackson?" My temper begins to rise with the blaze of the pretend fire.

I hear what sounds like a little-boy voice from my tall egret man, "Aren't you going to go with me?" he whimpers.

"Yes, Mr. Jackson, I will go with you! I am here and I will go with you!" Mr. Jackson and I walk side by side, neither touching the other. We eventually make it to the fire door. I have to turn my back on him, for I have more and more residents to rescue for the drill. Finally, weary caretakers are told that the drill is over and we shake our heads at the difficulty of a pretend fire on the Alzheimer's unit. We pray a real fire will never come our way.

But I find hope that the man who has never liked crowds and probably never will showed me the way out of the chaos. We must go together to escape the fire. During a crisis, if we walk side by side, we can make it to the door.

What Time Is It?

"What time is it?" she asks every time she can catch the attention of a staff member or another resident.

If she asks during the devotional time, I stop what I am doing and reply politely with the time from the clock above her head.

"Huh?" she says back to me.

"It is 2:35," I say a little bit louder so that she can hear.

"Oh--thanks." She seems at peace until she perks up again a minute later. "Is it Tuesday?" she asks innocently.

"It's Monday," I answer.

"You sure it isn't Tuesday? I could swear it's Tuesday."

A part of me wants to agree it is Tuesday because time has never been very important to me. But she really does want to know the day of the week. She is still halfway a part of this reality. She will ask many people and, if we do not agree, she will partially remember our different answers and become even more upset.

I go back to telling the small gathering the difference in my children's personalities and the What–time-is-it?-woman fades into the background once again. She closes her eyes and ignores my homily about God's diverse creation. Four minutes later she is awake again. "What time is it?" she asks as if she has never said those words.

I stop mid-sentence. "It's 2:40."

"Do we get something to eat?"

"Do you want something to eat?"

"It depends on what you have."

"I have peanut butter crackers," I offer. I know what is in the snack drawer in the nurses' station because we have played this scene many times before.

"That's fine. I'll take those. And bring me something to drink too, please."

I leave the room and retrieve a package of four peanut butter crackers. I come back to the day room with the snack and a cup of water.

"Thank you," says the What-time-is-it?-woman.

"You're welcome." I try to sound cheerful. Like everyone else, I have grown tired of taking care of her. Hers is a personality that wears us out. I refocus and summarize my last words before retrieving the crackers. Soon I am back into the rhythm of the homily.

"What time is it?" she breaks in after she has finished her water and crackers.

"2:49." I say.

"How long are you going to talk?"

"Another five minutes," I answer honestly. Her

interruptions have stretched out my meditation.

"I want you to go away," she tells me.

I try to explain my presence. "Normally I wouldn't bother you. But these other people in this room want me to tell them this story and to pray to God. Do you want to go to your room where it is quiet?"

"No. I like this chair. I'm not leaving."

"Okay." I say, beginning to feel defeated.

"What time is it?" she asks again.

"It's 2:50."

"Thank you."

For two years our relationship is like this. We don't get better or worse. But finding out the history of the What-time-is-it?-woman keeps my temper in check. Her chart tells me part of her life story. Her husband walked out on her and their son. She had to go to work at a bank that paid her very little. She didn't have any relatives to take her in; so she and her son moved in with her ex-mother-in-law. She never remarried. She was a member of the First Baptist Church. As I read further down the page, I see words that make my heart skip a beat. The chart says that her only son committed suicide when he was twenty-eight.

What time is it? I think to myself. What if time is murky water that pushes her down and sloshes up to her neck and into her mouth? What if time is that thing that takes her even further from her memories of her beloved? What time is it? What day is it? Will I ever see my son again? My church says I won't. They tell me he committed a sin too great for heaven. What do you say? This isn't the life I wanted. It is the life I get anyway. What time is it? What day is it? Why did these terrible things happen to me? I will never mention my secrets to you or anybody else. I will only ask you to bring me a cracker or two. In my heart of hearts all I want to know is how many days have passed since I last held my baby boy and will I ever see him again? Can anybody tell me what time it is? Can anybody help me? Why am I still alive? I don't want to be alone like this. Please, please give me the structure and compassion I need to make it through another day without my son. I don't ask for much. I just want someone to tell me what time and day it is. Will you be patient with me? What time is it? What day is it?

The Tough, Brilliant, Outspoken Agnostic

Sam let me know when we met what she thought of chaplains: "You're only good for bringing me popcorn for the Friday movie."

"Oh, I see," I replied with no clue on how to make her change her mind.

In her younger days Sam was a social worker in the New York City prisons. Sam was and is a tough, brilliant, outspoken agnostic. What can Sam need spiritually? Some days I have to step out of her way as she hobbles by, screaming incessantly at yet another resident that infuriates her. I duck and hope her cane doesn't hit me.

"Preacher, move out of the way so I can clobber that S.O.B." Sam hesitates for just a moment until she can get past me. She picks up her walking stick, swinging it above her head at the most recent offender—someone who probably wandered into her room and who Sam wants to make sure never comes in again.

A month into our relationship I remembered that my father, also agnostic, takes pride in his intelligence. It is his form of religiosity. Although Sam can no longer carry on the conversations she had known before the disease, she needs someone to know how much she has worked at her intelligence. She wants to move past the frustration that her cognition is not always available when her feelings are still true to who she has always been. Sam is afraid no one knows she is still smart in her heart of hearts.

I peek into the bedroom Sam rarely leaves these days except to complain that none of us are doing our jobs.

"What do you want? Don't ask me to come to church with you!" growls Sam when she sees me at her door.

"Well, I was thinking about how smart you are..." I begin cautiously.

"What do you have up your sleeve, preacher? I'm too old and too wise for your tricks."

I start back out the door. "Well, all right, but you are the smartest resident on the unit and I was wondering if you would be willing to critique my meditation each week during the devotional time?"

"Hmm. I am the smartest, so you got me there, and I don't have anything to do right now. Okay, I'll come with you. But I'm warning you, I'm a really tough grader." A wicked smile slips across her face and I wonder if I am ready to make myself so vulnerable to this tough, brilliant, outspoken agnostic.

Every Tuesday after that day Sam grades my meditations somewhere between so-so and pretty good. A few hours after the meditation Sam is wandering up and down the unit like a lost sheep. She catches my arm. "I can't find my Daddy. He is a roofer. He could be on any one of these roofs in town. Will you help me look for him, please?" When Sam snaps out of little-girl mode, she attempts to overthrow the nursing staff to get her elopement bracelet removed. (The elopement bracelet is an alarm that keeps dementia residents from leaving the unit. We never know when Sam's brain will turn her into a child looking for her daddy again.) Sam shows the other residents that they, too, are sporting the confining strip of plastic that holds the alarm on their wrists. Most of the residents in the day room look at their arms and see that Sam is correct. In no time Sam has created a mutinous atmosphere. The head of the unit walks over to Sam. Snip. Off comes Sam's elopement bracelet until she is ready to wear it again later that day.

Sam comes back to grading me each week. She shakes her head in disgust, wondering if anything she says will ever get through the young preacher's thick head. One Sunday I come to get Sam so that she can come to the auditorium with me. It is my turn to do the large service with residents from all over the building.

"Oh no, she won't want to go," says the innkeeper on Sam's floor.

"Yes, I do want to go because I've got work to do," Sam snarls.

I don't remember my sermon on that day but I remember Sam--for just as I concluded my homily, Sam arose and told the congregation in her loudest revolutionary voice, "She did it! That's my girl. I taught her to preach!"

A few months later her son moves her to another Alzheimer's unit in another part of the city. I catch Sam on her way out the door. I look at her standing in front of me with her head drooped and a tear slipping down her face. "Goodbye, preacher."

"Why don't you fight this?" I whine.

"Preacher, I don't have any fight left. I am an old woman and now I must go." She touches my cheek with her fingertips. I am stunned that she is really leaving. The elevator opens. Her son takes her arm and I take one last look at one of the bravest souls I know.

Trusting Each Other

Ruth is Jewish, a rare thing on this particular unit, which is filled with Methodists and Baptists. I have several Jewish friends in my personal life and I have a Master of Theology in Hebrew Bible. But none of that has helped me with Ruth. Her husband tells me he worries I will attempt to convert Ruth to Christianity. I explain that as a chaplain I am not allowed to proselytize and even if I was not a chaplain I respect the Jewish faith. He keeps a watchful eye on me nonetheless. I wonder how many before me have betrayed his trust. I offer to read to Ruth in Hebrew. I'm not great at it, but I have nine years of study behind me.

"No, thank you." both he and she say when I mention it. I find out that the local rabbi also makes little progress with Ruth. It is little consolation to me. I see her almost every day and he sees her quarterly. I limit my visits to short hellos and walks with her up and down the hall. I do not attempt to invade her thoughts.

I am told that Ruth was quite talkative when she arrived on the unit years ago. That is not the person I know. Sometimes she catches my arm and asks me something pertinent to her situation. I do my best to find answers for her. Ruth is a serious soul most of the time and when the rare moment arises to make her laugh she lets out a gutsy chortle. It is good to see her serious brow let go for a few minutes.

After a year Ruth no longer treats me with suspicion. We are more like neighbors that smile and wave to each other but we don't really know each other as well as we could. Ruth even drops in on story hour every once in awhile to chuckle at my family stories. She tells me hardly anything about her own family, just that she is pleased with them. Sometimes I feel somewhat sad for not making more progress with Ruth.

One day her husband admits that Ruth is growing more distant from him and asks if I could visit with her for him. I am surprised by his request but I honor it. While walking up and down the hall one day I say to Ruth, "How are things going with your husband?" She puts her arm on my shoulder and says, "I trust you more than any man these days. I can't explain it. I am sure I will come around again. But in the meantime this is just the way it is." I relay the information to her husband and he is glad that she is at least aware that he exists. He takes her out every day and soon she is back to appreciating him as the man she loves. After our talk I notice that Ruth gives me a hardier wave and a bigger smile when she sees me, although she doesn't offer any more words. I don't know what I have done right, other than to show respect and to take her seriously. There is so much more for me to know. In the meantime I just get lucky sometimes and that is enough for today.

In Their Hearts

I Love You

"I love you!" she blurts out, loudly enough so that everyone in the room can hear. We are in the middle of our weekly devotion on the Alzheimer's unit. She searches my eyes and chuckles to herself after her confession. We are holding hands, she and I, just as we do every week. You see, she usually fusses during my short meditation and that is when I slip my shy skin into her eager touch. The ritual hand-holding usually buys me another ten minutes to be with my other parishioners. Near the end of the extra time she either falls asleep or she finally succeeds in pulling me away from the gathered group of Alzheimer's residents.

On the devotional days that she doesn't fall asleep we leave the others behind in the big day room, my outstretched arm already following her as I try to make my goodbyes to those I am leaving behind. When my feet finally catch up to her, she walks me up and down the hall chattering on about things only she understands. She is a walker, a wanderer, and apparently she wants me to wander too.

So here we are in the devotional time once again. She is sitting in a comfortable cushioned chair fingering the veins in my left hand. I pause to recollect what I have been saying between the usual Alzheimer's unit interruptions. And that is when she makes her announcement--during one of my pauses that comes when I try to figure out why in the world I even attempt meditations at all. Maybe it doesn't sound like much, a simple "I love you" in the middle of all the chaos, but today it means a lot to me.

For two years she has mumbled to those of us who work with her. The main phrase that we have been able to decipher is, "Oh, it's you." I must admit there have been other times she has said, "I love you." And those times didn't touch me as much. I'm not sure why. Maybe it's history.

At the beginning of my relationship with her, her daughter told me she was just reacting to my emotions. That is why she liked me so much. She was mimicking me and borrowing from my upbeat style of chaplaincy. I thought I saw more. I thought I saw recognition of my individual person from her. Maybe it was wishful thinking on my part. Maybe I wanted to remain naive about her because I wanted to see only the good on the Alzheimer's unit.

A year later I missed a month of work because of a serious illness. I came back to the unit with very little energy. That first week of my return I walked sideways into her. I was exhausted and expressionless as I turned around to face her to apologize. Her eyes immediately lit up as she smiled and said while pointing towards me, "It's you!" Then her smile disappeared and she hit me on the arm and said, "Bad. Gone."

"Yes, I've been gone." I agreed. "But I am back now."

She chuckled and grabbed my hand. "Come on." She said as she pulled me up and down the hall for our familiar walkabout.

As we walked I contemplated that she had not mimicked me but had shown her own reactions to our situation. Her actions and words were separate and different from my own feelings of exhaustion.

Our relationship is two years old now. I don't see her as much these days because I have other duties. I still visit every now and then. It is during the devotional time today that she speaks to me. I am holding her hand as usual or she is holding mine as she soothes my calluses and scars. I have forgotten what I am talking about and I pause to collect my thoughts. She catches my eye with her insistent gaze before she speaks up.

"I love you," she says. Then she chuckles at her own declaration.

I grin before I put my forehead on hers and confess, "I love you, too."

She throws back her head and cackles from her soul.

That was it. No big band played, no heavenly hosts appeared. Just "I love you" from her to me and another "I love you" from me to her.

She told me she loved me, and this time I listened.

If Jesus Had Dementia

If Jesus had dementia, would he still be the Christ? Would he remember God is his "Abba"-Daddy? (Mark 14:36) his mother the Virgin Mary? Would he get lost on his way to heaven? What about his miracles? Could he still do them? If he could, would they be silly instead of serious? Would he create a blue-striped pig with a purple polka-dotted tummy?

One thing I know from working so long on the Alzheimer's unit: if Jesus had dementia, he would still love and be most honest. He would say, "You know, being me isn't an easy task, especially in this day and time. Sometimes I could swear I hear angels talking to me. Does that make me crazy?"

And I, his chaplain, would say, "You aren't crazy to me."

What if Jesus were to sin because of his dementia? Would we forgive him? Or would we say, "See there, I knew he deserved to be crucified! See there, what kind of savior would die and leave us behind in our pain?"

Perhaps it is silly to imagine Jesus with dementia, but I do know this: Some of the most respected people get Alzheimer's even though they have lived a good life. There are good mamas and good husbands and good sisters and good teachers and even good preachers with this disease. I suppose if Jesus had dementia, it would be sad, just as it is when our mentors and loved ones lose parts of their cognition.

Some days Jesus would remember things with such clarity. He would say, "I was a healer, wasn't I?" And I would agree. "Yes, you were a very good healer and you still are."

"I am?" the imperfect Jesus would say in surprise.

"Yes, for it is most healing to sit with you, now that you aren't so busy."

"I was busy, wasn't I?" Jesus would agree. "People came from near and far just to listen to my words. I must have been a great teacher."

"You were and still are," I would affirm, "for I can hear you much better without the crowds."

"Where are the crowds now?" Jesus would ask in all sincerity. "Don't lie to me, I can take it. I know you will tell me the truth. You always do."

I would have to hesitate and the sadness in his eyes would pierce me through. "Jesus, it isn't you. It's this society. It says that anyone who isn't perfect doesn't deserve to be loved, especially great leaders. We lift them up to knock them down. It keeps us from looking at our own pain and imperfections. But you already know this. You once said, 'Why do you see the speck that is in your brother's eye but you do not notice the log in your own eye?'" (Matthew 7:3)

"I said that?"

"Yes, and a lot of people took it to mean to try to be even cleaner and more perfect so they can get to pointing at their brothers and sisters once again."

"What about you? Do you think that is what it means? You are my preacher woman and I trust your opinion."

I would smile and say, "I took your words to mean, quit pointing and get to loving."

"I like that," Jesus would agree. "By the way, preacher, have you seen my mother? I can't find her this morning."

As usual my heart would break and I would say, "Your mother isn't here right now, but she knows where you are and she loves you."

He would sigh in discontent and resign himself to the reality that he gets me instead of his mother. Finally he would ask, "Preacher?"

"Yes, Jesus." I would answer softly.

"Preacher, I love you."

"I know, Jesus. You always have, and I love you, too."

"Will you visit me again, Preacher?"

"Of course I will. I will come back."

"Thanks."

And I would look back over my shoulder as I left him there in his chair. His image would haunt me just as they all do.

Chapter Two - Smiling

In Their Hearts

Smiling

Even though Alzheimer's is a devastating disease, not all is lost. There are still delightful times on the Alzheimer's unit. Some of these good times have to do with the individual residents who have always been able to have fun and see the positive in this world. These individuals continue to help the rest of us smile. Other wonderful times happen because of the disease itself. Somebody will say something he or she would never have said when that person had no dementia. One daughter told me that her father had always been critical of her mother. Now that her father had Alzheimer's disease, every day he told his wife he loved her and he rarely criticized her any more. Whatever the reason, there are a lot of good times to be had on the Alzheimer's unit and I am glad to have experienced so many of them.

In Their Hearts

Hey, Preach!

I have lived and worked in this city most of my life, but according to Tommy we are not in the city. We are in his small town in the southern part of our state. There is no arguing about it, no convincing him otherwise. We ARE in Tommy's hometown. There has never been a female preacher at Tommy's home church. He thinks I am the first. So he calls me "Preach" to fit his reality.

"Hey, Preach!" Tommy yells to me from down the hall. "Tell me something. Should I take the day off and hang out with you?"

I am glad to see Tommy's friendly face, "Sounds good. I've got to visit a couple of folks. Do you want to walk with me?" I ask.

"I'm coming," Tommy says as he hobbles to catch up. "Now listen here, Preach, some of these folks can be right ornery at this church. You just can't take it personally."

"I see," I answer seriously.

And now that Tommy has my ear, he tells me the same story he tells me every time he sees me. "You know, my daddy was head of finances and my mama was treasurer of this here church when I was a boy. Shoot, I've been counting offering all my life," Tommy chuckles to himself.

"Is that right?" I say, sounding surprised before I ask, "Since we are on the subject of church, are you coming to the church service today, Mr. 'I've Been Counting Offering All My Life'?"

"I'm thinking on it. But I can't make any promises." Tommy answers hesitantly.

"Okay, then, I'm knocking on your door at church time."

"You got it, Preach. I'll be seeing you."

"See you, Tommy."

"Take care of yourself, Preach. I mean it."

"I will."

In Tommy's hometown world my weekly devotion on the Alzheimer's unit is called a "church service" or "church" for short. Story time, also once a week, is more favored by Tommy than church, since he thinks he will have to count money. One day story time was labeled by Tommy to fit his reality. After an hour of hearty laughs at my stories, especially by Tommy, he arose and said to the room, "We'd like to thank the preacher for coming to our Elks Lodge meeting this month. Let's give her a round of applause and maybe we can get her to come back another time." And applaud they did. The other Alzheimer's residents followed Tommy's lead.

I think Tommy hated being a salesman most of his adult life because he rarely mentions it with pride as he does his family and friends. I think he survived his work with wit and humor just as he did most of the difficult things in his life.

One day during "church" I say, "Hey, Tommy, you got a favorite hymn you want to sing?"

Tommy smiles a crooked smile and says "I don't have a favorite him but I got a favorite her." His sides shake as he laughs the hardest at his own joke. The other residents and I can't help but laugh too. Tommy is funny. He brings humor to the tough situation of living and working on the Alzheimer's unit where people can be "right ornery."

Ten months into my ministry I was trying to do paper work in the office on the Alzheimer's floor. It is almost impossible to complete paperwork in such an active place. I attempted to catch up anyway. Tommy spied me and pulled up a chair next to the desk I was borrowing. "Um, Preach, I know you think you are doing something important there, but I need to talk to you."

I barely looked up from my work. I couldn't imagine what could be so important as to interrupt my required drudgery. I tried to ignore Tommy.

"Well, the thing of it is, Preach..." Tommy continued despite my refusing to give him my full attention. "The thing of it is that you are doing a right fine piece of work here at the church."

I dropped my pen and looked up.

The worn face in front of me continued. "Now, Preach, I'm not one to give out compliments lightly and I doubt I'll tell you again. You know when they said they were hiring a woman to be the preacher, I didn't know what to say. But I have to admit we made a good choice."

"Thank you, Tommy."

"You're welcome."

I admit I don't mind being the first woman preacher at the church in Tommy's hometown. The longer I am here the more I can feel the honor that Tommy has bestowed on me. In fact I am thinking of "sticking around for a while" as long as Tommy will have me.

Sneaking Candy

Most of the time she is quiet, not saying a word. It looks as if she is waiting for something or someone. If she is, I have never seen that person or event. Her mouth falls down into a frown. I suppose, if I didn't know her, the glare upon her face would frighten me. Tell her a story and she lights up like downtown Atlanta during the holidays. She slaps her thigh and laughs with glee. So different is she, I'm not sure it is the same woman. Because I have never met her family, I don't know if she has always been like this or if it is the disease. I suppose it is a little of both.

She is never a problem. She draws so little attention to herself in the room in which she has chosen to sit and stare into oblivion. She would get very little contact with others except for the activities that take place all day long. I call her name and her glare transforms into a grin. I am the story woman and if you interrupt me she will shush you. "Be quiet. I'm trying to listen here!" she barks at the story time offenders. And for a small moment she isn't so quiet after all. "You can go ahead." She coaxes me back to the story I am trying to retrieve from my brain that is still stunned at seeing a perfect mouse turn into a lion.

Melanie, the activity therapist, talks her into giving up her chair to go downstairs to cooking class.

I pull up a seat next to her at the table in the kitchen. "Hey, Rose," I say.

"Hey." She grins back for only a second, for something has caught her eye: m&m candies have been poured into a bowl between the two of us. Rose's gaze is locked in on the delectable treat. I watch Rose glance over her shoulder for some kind of invisible authority before she sneaks a handful of candy.

"I won't tell," I say, grabbing my own handful. "I think you've got a great idea."

Rose smirks and her shoulders shake to the rhythm of her giggling. She gobbles her handful and I follow suit. The only other time I have seen such joy in sneaking candy is in young children 1/16 of Rose's age. I cherish this small moment with her, knowing I will rarely see such glee from her the rest of this month, or even the next. To Rose's delight I continue to sneak candy with her while baking instructions are given.

Melanie spies our now-empty bowl. "Hey! Where did all the candy go?"

"I don't know," I tease and Rose giggles even more.

"Rose, did you eat up all the candy?" Melanie questions.

Rose's eyes plead for help from me.

"Now why would you say that?" I interfere.

Rose grins from ear to ear. We are suspiciously entrusted with a more limited serving of m&m's this time and of course we eat them too. I don't remember having so much fun like this in a long time. Plain ol' kid fun is what it is and always will be.

Now every time I see Rose glaring at the people around her I think of m&m candies and how much delight she took in sneaking them with me. After I wrote it, I read this story to Rose. I didn't tell her she was the subject. If she doesn't remember the particular incident, it could be more frightening than rewarding. And so I read this story to Rose and to the others on her unit. Afterwards I asked, "What do you think, Rose?"

Rose smiled with satisfaction, nodded her head and said, "It's your best one yet!"

Joy Rides and Field Trips

The two activity therapists, Melanie and Richard, take as many residents as possible on something called "joy rides". Joy rides are trips around the local neighborhood in the geriatric complex's van. There are other field trips to specific destinations such as to the famous Varsity drive-in for lunch or to Stone Mountain for a picnic. Joy Rides are not to a specific destination. They are a chance to just get away from the unit and have some fun. When I was young, my father called it "running some errands." He would say, "I've got some errands to run. Does anyone want to come with me?" I was always eager to run errands with Daddy because it really meant he would ride through the neighborhoods and just make sure Atlanta was still standing. In other words, the errands were few and the ride was wonderfully long and scenic. When we ran errands, my father shared his family and business experience that he thought would help me in my future adulthood. These days when I go on joy rides with the Alzheimer's residents, I am reminded of the days when I ran errands with my father.

One dreary overcast day I was telling stories in the day room when Melanie and Richard brought back a group of folks from a joy ride. These joy riders were added to my audience. One woman was grinning as she took her seat.

I asked, "Did you have a good time?"

She said, "Boy, did I! We went to Dee-troit!"

"You don't say." I responded in surprise that a van could zip from Atlanta to Detroit in an hour. I could see our new advertisement in my head: "Come to our Alzheimer's unit where our van can take you from Atlanta to Detroit and back in just one hour."

The joy rider in front of me brought me back to her reality. "Yes, Ma'am. We went to Dee-troit. I'm telling you Detroit is looking a whole lot better and cleaner than when I lived there. Makes me feel awful proud." She kept smiling and mumbling about "Dee-troit" and shaking her head in wonderment and sighing with pride for the rest of the hour. I remember feeling so happy for her. She had found joy in her context. She didn't go to the Detroit on your and my map but she got there in her own way. Seeing Detroit in a better condition seemed to bring good feelings. She was able to hold those good feelings close to her heart despite and because of her dementia. Do I think this disease is a blessing? No. I think that it robs individuals of too many things to call it a blessing. Yet I am amazed at how creative some persons with Alzheimer's disease can be to deal with their problems. This woman had remembered Detroit in her heart and, when she looked out the van window, she saw her old residence in a better light than she had ever known it in reality. The truth is this woman has "made good" with her life and all her children have become successful professionals. One is even a famous politician. She has come a long way from her childhood in Detroit and I don't just mean she has changed geographic locales. I think she saw Detroit in a better condition, because her own life is in a better condition. She has worked hard and has many reasons to be proud of herself. I think she saw a reflection of her own life when she looked out the window of the joy ride van.

Another similar situation involves not one person but two. I was invited by the activity therapists to go on a picnic to Stone Mountain. Julia Norman was one of the ten residents on the field trip. Sitting next to Julia on the van taking us to Stone Mountain was a woman who always seems to be lost. Many years ago she was the first dean of women at a well-known college. This woman is used to being in charge. The onset of Alzheimer's disease seems to have made her feel out of control and more distressed than most of the other residents. Perhaps it is because she has had more control to lose than most people. Julia Norman is also used to being in charge; only she feels no less in charge with her dementia. In Julia's opinion a few quick questions can clear up any matter. Sometimes she doesn't even need to ask questions to draw her unique conclusions. We had had a wonderful picnic at Stone Mountain. The staff was worn to the bone from all the excitement and work it takes to pull off such an event with Alzheimer's residents. No one seemed to be saying much of anything on the trip back to the unit.

The ex-dean broke the silence when she aasked, "Where are we? I seem to be lost." I sighed with the activity therapists because it was a question we were used to hearing all day. Our answers rarely helped her anxiety. But we had nothing to fear. Julia Norman would take care of the situation. She was sitting next to the ex-dean and perked right up. Julia looked out over metropolitan Atlanta. Julia was raised in South Carolina but she lived her adulthood in Tennessee. After taking in the landscape outside the van Julia announced in an authoritative voice no one could dispute, "Well, Darling, we're in Tennessee. I don't recognize this particular neighborhood, but it's Tennessee all right!"

"Why, thank you," said the ex-dean and she was satisfied for the next five minutes until she asked once again where she was. Yet again Julia Norman pointed out that we were in Tennessee. At one time the ex-dean would have needed to know that we were really in Atlanta but Julia showed us that at this point in the disease she really wanted to know who was in charge.

Julia, ever ready to take the reins, was able to calm her seatmate over and over again better than any staff member. Julia's sense of well-being and philosophy spread over the van. Things were going to be all right, as Julia's authoritative voice let us know. According to Julia Norman, if we don't recognize the neighborhood, we aren't completely lost. We are just a short distance from home. And with that small scrap of good news we all breathed a little bit easier.

In Their Hearts

Pumpkin Shopping

Just before Halloween, Melanie and Richard, the activity therapists, decided to take six residents to pick out pumpkins that they would later decorate. I was invited to share in the fun. The gooey insides of the pumpkins would also make sweet yummy pies and the seeds would be baked and salted for a fun snack. Our destination was just a short distance down the road where the van from our geriatric complex delivered us to a fenced-in churchyard. At first glance it looked as if we had found the supplier of all the basketballs in the NBA. Apparently an entire pumpkin farm had been transported to this one tiny patch of grass in the suburbs. The six Alzheimer's residents knew what to do. They immediately began to roam freely up and down the rows. The part of their brains that had to do with round orange plant life had not been lost. While Melanie and Richard had taken on their tasks as activity therapists by looking for paintable pumpkins, I watched my six elderly friends stroll the rows of the transported farm with a warm glow of yesteryear. The wind whipped the tall groaning oaks that also seemed to be watching these six revived souls with rosy cheeks. Wrinkled hands thumped, and massaged, and pressed, and thumped again. Finally the six Alz-heimer's residents had each chosen a pumpkin or two and then nestled their fire-colored babies into six sets of arms.

When it came time to pay, Melanie politely asked the prices of the different sized pumpkins that she and the residents were clutching. The woman who had volunteered to sell the pumpkins that hour was trying to raise money for the church's youth group. I was not surprised to hear that the small pumpkins were two to three dollars each and the larger pumpkins were six to eight dollars. But Julia Norman caught wind of the prices and was outraged.

"What!?" she exclaimed as she stepped between Melanie and the seller, a pumpkin under each arm. "Why that's highway robbery. We will pay no such thing!"

There were no words about Alzheimer's disease or dementia on the outside of our van and we had not felt a need to explain it to the seller for such a short outing. So the woman volunteer did not know that Julia lived in her own reality. Melanie attempted to break back into the conversation with an explanation but Julia still had the floor. "We'll pay you half as much." Julia snapped out the words like a general to a private. "And that is still more than we should spend. Why, you're making a killing off of us."

To everyone's surprise the seller reluctantly mumbled, "Okay, it's a deal."

Julia Norman sighed impatiently and said, "That's more like it."

Melanie pulled out the cash as Julia watched her count out each and every penny.

As we were getting back on the van, I turned to Julia and said seriously, "I ought to take you shopping with me, since you are so good at knocking down prices."

Julia Norman patted me on the back, "Be glad to help out any time, my dear. You know where I live." As usual she was right.

Bingo

A successful sister of one of the dementia residents brought her office mates to the unit one afternoon to lead several games of Bingo. I was sitting at a table with Julia Norman, the woman from Detroit, and the woman who used to sing[9].

Every time a number was called out, the woman from Detroit would yell "Bingo!" which would make the successful business folks think she had won the game. I would then explain it wasn't really a Bingo.

And Julia Norman would say, "Oh brother. Honey, don't you even know when you have a Bingo?"

Round and round it went with the woman from Detroit yelling "Bingo" yet again, the suit and tie business folks thinking she had won, my explaining it wasn't really a Bingo, and Julia Norman throwing in an "Oh brother" loud enough for the entire room to hear. I was trying not to laugh because this cycle was beginning to irritate some of the suits and ties. I looked across the table and the woman who used to sing was removing her clip-on earrings to use them as markers on her Bingo card. This was too much for me. I couldn't hold back my giggles.

---

[9]The story about the woman who used to sing is in Chapter Four.

Julia Norman leaned over and scolded, "Stop that! Stop giggling at those strange looking Bingo people. You might hurt their feelings. They are trying real hard to carry this thing off and you aren't helping."

I agreed and kept my giggles to myself after that.

When "B-3" was called, the woman from Detroit yelled "Bingo!" yet again.

I automatically snapped at her, "You don't have a Bingo!"

"Yes, I do!" she insisted.

I looked at her card to check out her claim. For once she really did have a Bingo. It was hard to believe but it was true. I told the folks running the game that she really did win this time. The woman from Detroit received some nicely wrapped soaps and held her sweet-smelling basket of goodies high enough for all to see.

"I told you I had a Bingo," the woman from Detroit said as she wagged her finger at the businessman who had given her the prize moments earlier.

"Oh brother," said Julia Norman. "You'd think she's never had a Bingo in her whole life."

The woman who used to sing moved her earrings around her own Bingo card and looked at me for approval.

"Looks great!" I agreed.

I don't know if those folks from the sister's office will ever lead another Bingo game on the Alzheimer's unit. But I can say some of us had a wonderful time.

When Jesus Comes To Town

When Jesus comes to town, he visits the Alzheimer's Unit because it's the best place to be. He starts his day by playing Go Fish with Miss Bessie. Then he relates a tale to Big Tommy and Victor from Kalamazoo. Later he gobbles up all the leftover chocolate candy with Sue from Sassafras Tea, Kentucky. When he gets tired he throws his legs up on the screen porch rail and rocks to the beat of his own creation.

"Wow, look at that sky!" he says to Mr. Roger Smith while time stands still.

After a wonderful lunch of lemon chicken and green beans with Lucy, Miss Mary and Donald Demetree, Jesus wanders aimlessly into devotion to sing all those hymns from way back when.

Sometimes he has to stop and weep and sigh over another lost lonely lamb crying for his or her mommy. "Oh, how I wish they didn't know such pain, but you know we live in an imperfect world and pain is going to be with us until we all get to heaven."

Jesus also blesses all the families and caregivers. He gives them strength and imagination to make it through one more day of this dreaded disease-- this disease that robs them of their loved ones and their life energy.

I tell you these things because I have already seen Jesus on the Alzheimer's Special Care Unit each and every day. I have seen him in you and in me. I have seen us do the things I mention here. They are not abstractions from my imagination. But we are not the only ones who carry Jesus to the Alzheimer's unit. I have seen Jesus in the residents who live behind locked doors. I have seen persons with dementia of the Alzheimer's type show love, and more love. They show love to me, to each other, to their families and to their caretakers. We will reap spiritually what we sow. Love is patient. Love is kind. But most of all love never ends. (Galatians 6: 7-8, I Corinthians 13: 4,8) It never ends and, if we love when we are cognitive, we will love again and again. Just ask Jesus the next time you visit the Alzheimer's unit. I'm pretty sure he'll be there, because the Alzheimer's Unit is the best place to be.

Chapter Three - Going

In Their Hearts

Going

The Neuro-Psych unit at the geriatric hospital is where persons with Alzheimer's disease (and other types of dementia) go to be observed and evaluated by psychiatrists. Sometimes Alzheimer's contributes to anxiety, depression, aggression and other complications associated with memory and communication losses. The Neuro-Psych unit is where behaviors and moods can be monitored as different medications are tried to ease the suffering of the patient. Also, at any time during the progression of the dementia an individual can develop harmful behavior toward self and/or others. That person will get moved to the Neuro-Psych unit for a week or two. In short, when people ask what the Neuro-Psych unit is, I tell them it is where you go when you hit somebody. That may sound funny, but that is one of the reasons people end up getting evaluated on the Neuro-Psych unit. It is the Alzheimer's Special Care Unit turned on high. People live on the Alzheimer's special care unit the rest of their lives and are called residents. They visit the Neuro-Psych unit for a week or two and are called patients. Eighty residents on the Alzheimer's Special Care Unit live there permanently. A different group of twenty people live in a small observation area on the Neuro-Psych unit. The professionals who work there never know who or what they will see each day on the Neuro-Psych unit.

The move to the different environment of the Neuro-Psych unit is disconcerting for the dementia population. Imagine your surroundings magically changing. Many dementia patients don't remember how they got to the hospital. This abrupt change adds fear to the confusion they are already experiencing. Some of the people I meet on the Neuro-Psych unit are the same people I already know from the Special Care Alzheimer's unit. I am thankful that I get to go with my residents to the Neuro-Psych unit in their time of crisis. Other folks are new to me and I am new to them. Either way, Neuro-Psych patients, families and staff are thankful for the presence of chaplains. I am the week-day chaplain on the unit. Other chaplains come by in the evenings and also lead a worship service on Sunday afternoons. I am thankful for the help from my colleagues. I can't imagine working on the Neuro-Psych unit all day the way the nurses do. I come in for only one hour each day, which is enough "turned on high" for me.

She Taught Me to Dance

I like her. I mean I really like her. My first month on the unit, Lizzy taught me to dance. We were at the Big Band Ball in the auditorium. She grabbed my hand and said, "Come on, let's dance!"

I tried to plant my feet firmly on the ground. "I'm not very good at dancing," I protested like an insecure teenager.

"Who cares?" Lizzy shot back over her shoulder as she pulled my reluctant body to the center of the floor. The truth was Lizzy wasn't much of a dancer either, but she beamed from ear to ear as she grooved to the music in her own special way.

"I'm sorry I'm not very good at this," I apologized again and again.

"Are you having fun?" she called to me over the music.

"Yes," I had to admit. Who could resist the sparkle in Lizzy's eye, full of hope, wonder, and life?

"Good! That's all that counts," she assured this new chaplain. "We're here to have fun." At that moment I could swear Lizzy was a young woman, if it wasn't for her aging skin. Who knows? Maybe this was her chance to live again or maybe this was how she always has been.

After the dance she couldn't find her room. I took her by the hand and led her home.

"Thank you," she smiled in gratitude as she patted me on the head as if I were a child.

Every time I saw Lizzy after that, my feet did a little jig. She would chuckle and tap out a few steps of her own. Her words continued to tease and play with the perfectionistic workaholic in my head. "We're here to have fun! We're here to have fun! Nanny-Nanny-Boo-Boo! We're here to have fun!"

After I had known Lizzy for a year, her teasing had begun to go too far with some of the other residents. She had lost her adult boundaries. First Lizzy dared someone to push another resident out the window. Fortunately on the Special Care Alzheimer's Unit the windows don't open wide enough for anybody to get out of them. The incident was recorded on Lizzy's chart and she was watched a little more closely after that. Then for some reason Lizzy, who wears a size-14 dress, continuously accused her size-6 roommate of stealing her clothes. Though it sounds ridiculous to the rest of us, sometimes dementia has no reason. Two months ago the clothes jealousy led to Lizzy's second event. She pulled her roommate onto their bedroom floor by tugging at the other woman's sweater.

Lizzy was sent to the Neuro-Psych part of the geriatric hospital. It was a legal thing. The doctors had to figure out how to curb her aggressive behavior. A few weeks later a walking zombie in Lizzy's body stumbled back onto the Special Care Alzheimer's Unit. She was given a new room and a new roommate. Ever so slowly the drugs were reduced. Lizzy's pushing and pulling have apparently stayed at the hospital's Neuro-Psych unit while the good in Lizzy is back to delight us all. That special sparkle has crept back into her eyes and I am pleased.

"Lizzy" I exclaimed at the beginning of this month. "Are you okay?"

"Of course I'm okay." Her old wry smile worked hard to claim her face.

Things have gone well ever since. I am 18 months into knowing and dancing and giggling and playing with Lizzy. And then today I found out her family is moving her to an Alzheimer's unit closer to their home. She is leaving this very day--the same day I have found out about her departure. She won't be coming back. I wish they wouldn't move Lizzy. But I am the chaplain. I am not family. Residents come and residents go. Only--I like her. So today I will grieve the loss of the woman who taught me how to dance.

In Their Hearts

Pudding in My Pocket

Lately he follows me as if I have pudding in my pocket or a salad in my shoe. Maybe it's Jell-O in my jacket or a hot dog in my hair. But I don't have any of those things. I don't have gold or candy or a sunken treasure either. I just have me. It remains a mystery to me as to why George brightens, stands up straight, and follows me down the hall and back up again. I don't know if he knows I am his chaplain or if I am just the woman that brings that "down home" feeling. Because I feel most welcome and at home on the Alzheimer's unit, I think those feelings trickle out here and there onto George. Maybe that is why he follows me. But George doesn't tell me what he sees in me. Instead he smiles with his eyes and he takes my hand and we are off again.

But I know I am George's chaplain yesterday, today, and tomorrow. And my heart breaks for him. He has been temporarily moved from the Alzheimer's Special Care Unit because he has been hitting other residents. He needs to be observed at the hospital by doctors and nurses and case-workers and everyone else in the Neuro-Psych observation area. Neuro-Psych at the hospital is my assignment too. When I arrive for the devotional time I find George wandering in uncharted territory.

I stop in front of him and catch his roving vision. "Hey," I say, "do you remember me? I am Mary Margaret, your chaplain."

A light turns on in George's head. He looks deeply into my curious eyes. "Of course I remember you! Why would I not remember you?!"

I have wounded his pride and I regret asking something that hurts him so. "Do you want to come over here and sing some hymns with me?" I ask in chaplain-ese trying to make it up to him.

"I don't know. I'm not a very good singer," he replies reluctantly.

"Oh, you don't have to sing well to be with me."

"Well, if you put it that way, I will come and sing with you." His smile creeps up on me.

And we sing and we sing. George, some others, and I sing hymns we remember singing with our grandmothers long ago. We sing from our souls and from our toes. But when it is time to go I see fear in George's eyes. Is it a fear of getting lost in the obscurity once again? Or of losing all his sacred memories that belonged only to him? Parts of George are snatched away each day by a low-life bandit camped in his brain. Lately the bandit has been unplugging connections faster than they can be made. There is nothing I can do about it. No matter what, George's brain is in decay.

Oh, sweet loving George, who takes my hand and sings with me, Oh, sweet loving George, who trusts me so, how can I help you?

He follows me as if I have pudding in my pocket or a salad in my shoe. Maybe it's a Jell-O in my jacket or a hot dog in my hair. But I don't have any of those things. I don't have gold or candy or a sunken treasure either. I just have me. Somehow that is enough for George and others like him. Is it enough for me? Is it enough for me? Is it enough for me?

In Their Hearts

The Principle of the Matter

"Who are you?" She points her long narrow index finger into my shoulder like a soldier questioning a prisoner. Her six-foot frame casts a shadow over me.

"I'm Mary Margaret. I'm the chaplain around here."

"A chaplain, you say? And what does a chaplain do?" Francine looks me over suspiciously as she has for the last eight weeks since she arrived on the Special Care Alzheimer's Unit. She has yet to remember my face.

"I'm a preacher." I remember that the word "preacher" makes more sense to Francine, and the other dementia residents, than the word "chaplain."

Francine continues her inquisition. "So you are a preacher. How do I know you are telling me the truth?"

"Well, I guess you don't," I admit. "but they do make me wear this badge with my picture on it. I think it is a pretty good one."

"Hmm. It'll do." Francine stares into my eyes as if they will tell her everything she wants to know. "A woman preacher, how about that? Well, you just lucked up. I happen to like women preachers." With that pronouncement Francine finally begins to smile.

"You do?" I am surprised that the line of questioning is cut short because of my gender.

"Sure do," says Francine. "Men only got one thing on their minds. So I think all the preachers in all the churches should be women. What do you think about that, Preacher-Woman?"

"I think that is a rather unique argument for women preachers."

"Ya' got that right. Now when do I hear you preach?" It's more of a demand than a question.

"Right now if you like. I'm going into the room right behind you and you are definitely invited to come along."

"You don't say. Well, let's get this here prayer meeting a-going," prompts the newest member of my congregation.

Francine's husband visits in the middle of our "church" gathering. He is glad to see his loved one happy and so he joins us too.

Francine is her name and Francine is what she goes by. That is what she tells you if you ask her. I remember the first time I saw her. She was wandering aimlessly around the Neuro-Psych unit at the geriatric hospital. She was looking for Joe, her husband. Francine was confused and lonely and she made my heart so sad. That was two months ago. Now she has acclimated as a resident on the Special Care Alzheimer's Unit. She is no longer searching for Joe. She knows he will arrive on the unit every day around

3:00, and lean over and kiss her on the cheek. In the summer he brings fresh fruit and vegetables from his garden or a roadside stand on his way to town from their country home. "Preacher, you got to try one of these." He coaxes me to eat yet another treat.

I don't regret it. I take a seat next to Joe and Francine when the devotional time has ended. They are from the hills of Tennessee originally. And he is ever so proud and still very much in love with his strong mountain woman. As soon as I peel my tangerine, Joe starts in on a story about Francine. "Preacher, I ever tell you about the time Francine talked a judge out of a speeding ticket?"

"Nope. I don't know that one," I admit, spitting a seed into my napkin.

"Well, see here, Francine was caught doing 80 on a long trip home one day. And she told the officer she would see him in court. You see, she refused to pay the ticket. So the next week Francine is standing in front of the judge with the trooper testifying against her. Then the judge gave Francine a chance to speak.

"She said, 'Your honor, I don't deny I was speeding. But it wasn't like I was the only one. The officer picked me out of a pack of about ten cars. If I had slowed down I would have caused a wreck. Now I think it is only fair you either ticket all of us who were speeding or you rip up my ticket. It's the principle of the matter. It isn't right to ticket only one of the cars in the middle of an entire group of speeding automobiles.'

"Well, sir, that judge said Francine made good sense and he tore up her ticket right then and there. He agreed it was the 'principle of the matter.'"

Francine perks up in the seat next to her husband. "Well, it was the principle of the matter! That patrolman shouldn't have ticketed me unless he was planning on ticketing the whole lot of us."

All three of us laugh out loud. I am glad I know someone as strong and argumentative as Francine. I can see why Joe is so proud of his strong mountain woman. And I don't mind having a fan of women preachers even if the reason is a politically incorrect one. After all, it's the principle of the matter. The judge was on Francine's side long ago and now I don't mind that Francine is on mine.

The Lady with the Red Bible

Miss Ruby Sue carries her red Bible in her right hand. Her middle finger saves the place where she was reading before she heard me singing with the other patients in the Neuro-Psych part of the hospital. Miss Ruby Sue decides to join our small gathering.

Soon she is proclaiming, "Praise the Lord" between singing ol' hymns she knows better than I do. This is my first and last time to meet this unique woman. She is only passing through. Soon Miss Ruby Sue is testifying about her Jesus. The spirit has come upon God's servant in a way that makes some of the staff uncomfortable but there is no stopping her now. The other patients are riveted by Miiss Ruby Sue's charisma. They show they understand this way of doing church by throwing in an "Amen" or two when they can.

Ruby Sue waves the scriptures above her head and asks for a "Hallelujah." She tells her tiny congregation, of which I have now become a part, that we must be saved to enter the pearly gates. Ruby Sue's glasses slide down her nose. She is covered in sweat. Ruby Sue looks half-wise and half-disheveled. I want her to push her glasses back in place so that they don't fall off her face, but Miss Ruby Sue cannot be interrupted for such earthly concerns at this time. She tells us we are all related as God's children and God's grace is enough for us. Miss Ruby Sue breaks into song in the middle of testifying. She sings, "I've got a telephone in my bosom that God will answer any time. All I've got to do is call."

I leave Ruby Sue with her flock "Amen"-ing and clapping to her sermon. I decide that I am no longer needed at this particular site because Miss Ruby Sue is the preacher today. I am glad that dementia has not taken away her ability to testify--the most important thing to her. It may not be the way I do church but I am not here for me. Miss Ruby Sue is happy and more than surviving the observation at the geriatric hospital. She has proven she has a spiritual strength that cannot be broken by a decaying brain; I can testify to this good news. I was there and saw this event with my own eyes and ears. And I felt the spirit of God, too.

I Wish I Could Go Away

Today at the Neuro-Psych unit, a woman I had never met before walked right up to me and placed her hand in mine. She looked me in the eye and talked to me as if she had always known me when she said, "I wish I could go away with you. We could have others wait on us all day."

"Sounds good to me," I confessed to the mystery woman who knew my soul.

She giggled at my honest reply.

Today I was also training a chaplain intern to help me with my work. I said to the intern, "Look, I already made a new friend."

"Is it any wonder?" the intern said without hesitation.

What does that mean? Does it mean dementia patients will love anybody, especially on the Neuro-Psych unit? Or does it mean the new patient can tell how much I already like being with her? I don't know the answer to my questions. Such wisdom is beyond me. I've been a chaplain almost two years now. My specialty has been in Alzheimer's. But I am not any closer to why so many patients like me. Most of the people I work with can't give me answers to such questions. If I were to ask, "Why do you like me?" what would the woman want to say but can't find the words to any more? Is it because I am here in the trenches with you, or can you see my heart, too?

"Hey, Jesus" (I pray inside my mind), "what do you say? Do you like me? If you do like me, is it because I am here in the trenches with you? Or do you see my heart too? Does anyone else understand how difficult it is for me to be out and about with other people with my Asperger's Syndrome? How do I explain me? Why am I a minister today? Am I really helping anybody? I wish I could go away more often and taste a bit of heaven. I wouldn't mind having others wait on me all day every once in a while. Oh, Jesus, do you like me?"

Do You Want to Pray?

One Friday I arrived at the Neuro-Psych unit to lead the weekly devotion. The devotional time takes a different form each week because the small congregation is ever changing. I usually begin with hymn-singing and see what develops from there. As I walked over to the most populated area of the unit, I was followed by a woman who was moaning and patting her chest. She began circling me as she continued to moan and pat. "Ooooh Ooooh!"

"Would you like to come and sing hymns with us?" I asked, pointing to the rest of the patients sitting in a small circle of chairs.

"Oooooh!" Pat, pat, pat. "Oooooh! Yes!" She answered before she took a seat next to me. The woman attempted to sing the hymns. But three minutes later she was up again. She was back to moaning and patting her chest as she circled the rest of us.

Once again I asked if she wanted to join us and once again she did.

This pattern of joining us for a few minutes before going back to pacing, patting and moaning continued for the entire half-hour of the devotion. I had no idea who this woman was and I had no idea how to help her. I had not read her chart; therefore I didn't know anything about her spirituality. I usually read charts after my initial meeting with patients so that I can put a face to the person written about in the chart. So, all I knew was this woman before me appeared to be a tormented soul. Although it wasn't the first time I had met someone like her, her moaning was beginning to bother me because she was pacing right next to my head.

Finally the devotional time was over and I was ready to go. The woman followed me to the other side of the unit. She reached out and grabbed my arm with a vice grip that wasn't going to let go any time soon. "Please. Please," she said between the moans and patting.

We stood there like that for some time. I was perplexed. I had no idea what she wanted. Then I offered something I rarely offer. Chaplains are not supposed to proselytize our patients. We are supposed to give patients and residents the spirituality that they request from us. Unlike being a pastor of a church where the congregation's beliefs are usually somewhat similar, chaplains spend time discovering the spirituality of their parishioners in a pluralistic world. Since my parishioner could not tell me what she needed with words, I decided to guess. I asked, "Do you want me to pray?"

She replied like a child offered candy. "Oh, yes! Yes!"

I took her by the hand and we sat down next to each other. I prayed, "Jesus, please release my sister from her suffering. It is so painful to see her moan in such agony. We know you have the power to do all things. Amen."

And the woman said, "Amen." She looked me in the eye and said, "Thank you. My name is Dorothy. I am Baptist. I am from a small town in south Georgia. I am so glad you came. Thank you for figuring out I needed prayer. Prayer has always calmed me. I have always believed in the power of prayer. These days it's like I get caught in a nonverbal loop and prayer seems to be one of the ways to release my tongue."

I replied in shock, "You can talk! You can say whole sentences!"

Dorothy said, "Sure. I can say a lot of things when somebody prays for me. Please do come back and pray for me again. You will, won't you?"

"Okay," I agreed, still in shock. Then I walked over and read her chart where there was no mention of prayer. I wrote in her daily notes, "Prayer works for Dorothy! She went from moaning to talking when I prayed for her."

That was the day Dorothy taught me there is more than one way to ask for prayer.

Chapter Four - Crying

In Their Hearts

Crying

The first time I visited a dementia resident on her deathbed, she said to me, "Don't leave me alone." She was aware that she wanted comfort and love in her last hours. She wanted me to sit by her side and wait for her last breath. This chapter is my record of scenes of the suffering and death of Alzheimer's residents. In these situations I learned to be still and let death come. I wasn't always patient or at peace when individuals died. I learned to sit, nonetheless. I learned to sit by each person's side and to hold hands. I learned to pray, to sing, and to love. These are some of the most sacred moments of my life.

In Their Hearts

Don't Leave Me Alone

"You might want to look in on Rachel," Alice, the floor nurse, mentions to me without looking up from her paperwork.

"Why?" I stop in my tracks, surprised that a nurse even knows I exist. In the three weeks I have worked on the unit I have noticed that the nurses and certified nursing assistants are very busy with the requirements of their jobs. Alice looks me hard in the eye. "She's dying."

I thank her and gather Melanie, the activity therapist, who has known Rachel longer than I have. We find Rachel tossing from side to side in her bed. "Rachel, we are here with you," we say, announcing our arrival.

"Don't leave me alone!" Rachel pleads and grips our hands. "Please don't leave me alone!"

"We won't leave you alone. We are here," I agree.

"We are right here beside you," Melanie adds.

"I've got to go!" moans Rachel.

"Go where?" I ask.

"I've got to go." Rachel says yet again.

"Rachel, do you have to go to the bathroom?"

"No. I've got to go!" Rachel is losing patience with me.

"Rachel, do you have to go see Jesus?" The truth is finally dawning on me. Melanie has already told me that Rachel is a devout Baptist. Rachel hasn't initiated her own spiritual conversations for months, but she still blurts out her opinions during the devotional time when her favorite topics show themselves. Some of her memory may be going but she hasn't forgotten her Jesus when she hears his name.

She responds to my present question about her savior. "Yes. Do you see him? He's in the clouds there. Do you see him?"

"Who, Rachel, who do you see?" I ask looking in the direction her finger is pointing.

"He's calling to me. Do you see him?" asks Rachel lost in her vision of Him.

"You mean Jesus?" I say dumbfounded.

"Of course I do," answers Rachel without a doubt in her dying mind. "I've got to go," she continues. "Can you go with me?"

I say nothing at first as I try to digest what Rachel is telling me. Finally, I concede, "I can hold your hand, Rachel, but you'll have to go to Him by yourself. I can't go with you on this trip. But I can sit here with you until you go."

As Rachel continues to point to Jesus and tell us she has to go, we sing her favorite hymns and we pray.

We wipe sweat from her brow. Her family cannot come yet. We are her family until they arrive.

"I love you but I've got to go," Rachel tells us.

"It's okay to go, Rachel," I whisper in her ear.

Melanie leaves for the day. I will stay a little longer.

"Rachel was a sweet soul," says Rachel to me.

"Yes, she is. Rachel is one of the sweetest souls I know," I say even though I haven't known her long.

"Thank you." Rachel smiles one of the last smiles in her lifetime. "He's calling to me and I've got to go."

When Rachel stops talking, I go home, sleep little and come back again the next morning.

Her words are gone. Her breathing is labored. Her eyes are trying to close.

I kiss her forehead and shed a tear. "Oh, Rachel, you were such a sweet soul."

And then her breath didn't come anymore. It packed its bags and moved to another place. Will a pair of new parents name their baby girl Rachel today? Oh, Rachel, can you see Jesus now? All she wanted was to not die alone. We held her cold hands, kissed her sweaty brow, sang her favorite hymns, and prayed for ourselves.

Who are we that we are allowed such sacred work? I noticed Rachel waited until morning to die. She did not die in the middle of the night. Was it so I could learn about life and death? Was that Rachel's gift to me?

Chaplain, hold my hand into death and I'll teach you how to live. You live by loving the least of these my brothers and sisters. You live by loving. (Matthew 25:40)

When the Spirit Dies

I have learned to sit quietly as death comes--not to make a scene. After all, I am a chaplain and I am there to comfort, not to be comforted. I hold their hands into death and I kiss their foreheads as they are freed from this life into the next. I rationalize that for as many that are released from their bodies there are new folks to take their place in my heart.

But today the angel of death is swooping down for one I want to protect and never let go of as long as I live. I call her "my Holy Spirit" because of her words my first week on the Alzheimer Special Care Unit. Nine months ago as I fumbled to tell a story to residents with dementia, a woman on the front row began to chant that I was stupid. I was so flabbergasted I couldn't think of anything to say. I wanted to go home.

And then a tender voice from the corner said, "Go ahead. Tell your story. People are like that around here all the time." I looked over at a woman who looked as old as Abraham's Sarah. She smiled a half-smile and went on in her wisdom, "I'm listening. What happened next at your grandmother's? Don't worry about what anyone says. Just tell your story." Then she winked her magic towards me. From that moment, with her kind words tickling my ears, I was able to pick up and create a favorite storytelling time for many of the residents and for me, too.

Every Wednesday my Holy Spirit woman attends the story hour more faithfully than she attends the devotional time on Mondays. She comes dressed with her wry smile and sparkling blue eyes. She can't tell you my name but she knows my soul. "Oh no, don't go yet. Just one more story. Perty please, will ya stay, please?" She coaxes me into ten more minutes of storytelling each week as no one else can. When I finally leave for the day she says, "I am so glad you came!" She forgets what she did a few minutes ago but she doesn't forget the heart of the stories or the face of this storyteller.

Tonight she is in the hospital and her breathing is not quite right. I never thought about my Holy Spirit woman dying, but she is. Her children have arrived from all over the country from places like Colorado and Chicago. The nurses shake their heads. They sense her time is near. I hunt for her hospital room even though I don't want to see her like this. Her daughters and nurses are amazed that she lights up when I come to visit. I am not so amazed. I am sad.

"Tell me another story and I can rest," she begs when she sees me.

"My grandmother had wild kittens that she fed..." I begin pushing back the tears.

"Oh, I love that one," she interrupts with glee.

"I love you," I say.

"I know you do, honey, and I love you too, but I am tired now. Tell me a story and I will go to sleep to the sound of your voice."

"Oh God, don't take her," I pray selfishly. "I don't want to lose this part of my heart. But, God, I know you need her. You must be missing your Holy Spirit. She did her job well. She taught me to listen to the good voices and to tune out the bad. I have a bit of advice for you, God. When you are feeling down, hang around with her some and you will feel much better. When you don't know what to say, she'll let you tell the same story again and again and again. If you try to be there for her, she will be there for you. I doubt I did as much for her as she did for this new chaplain. So go ahead and take her, but please remember I need another sweet loving spirit as beautiful as she is to sit in her chair and to wink at me."

The Southern Hostess

Her face is purple, yellow, maroon--colors a face shouldn't be. It pains me to see her this way.

"What happened?" I ask.

"What happened to whom?" asks sweet southern Lily. She has no memory of her fall.

Melanie, the activity therapist, fills me in. "Lily fell face-first last Friday. There was blood everywhere and she had to go to the emergency room."

"Oh, Lily!" I exclaim, imagining the pain.

"Isn't that somethin'!" she replies.

And my heart cries, "O God, it isn't fair! Why do persons with dementia forget how to walk? Unlike toddlers, they don't bounce back when they fall. Where is the grace for them? Where are you, God?"

"Dearest Mary Margaret, I'm right here in your heart, in your vision, in your writing, and in your touch. I have not left you just because Lily has known pain."

Sweet southern Lily takes me by the hand. "Come on, darlin'. Let's go for a walk."

We walk down the hall, but I am far from complaining to God. I think, "I don't know how much more heartbreak I can take. I'm not you, God. I never was. I never will be. Some days I just can't take any more pain on their part."

"Dearest Mary Margaret, you cannot be an excellent caretaker until you take care of yourself. Lily needs you to tend to your own bruises as you tend to hers."

Lily points to the elevator, "Let's go this way, honey." So we take a walk outside. Lily chatters on about this and that. Though I recognize most of her words, I have no idea what she is saying, partly because she speaks in mixed up riddles like most Alzheimer's residents. But mostly my mind is somewhere else.

I have floated back to my world inside of me. "God, it's hard for me to take care of myself," I admit reluctantly.

"Dearest Mary Margaret, I'm still here for Lily and for all my dear people. And that includes you. I am here. I'm not going anywhere."

"I want to believe you," I whine to God. "I really do. Only why can't I see you? Where are you?"

"Dearest Mary Margaret, I am in Lily and I am in you. I am not as far away as you make me out to be. I am here crying with you and for you and for Lily. I am here. I always will be."

Lily grabs my hand and says, "Come on, darlin'! We've got so much to do. Don't just stand there. Come along."

That's the way it is with God, and Lily, and me. We make it through yet another day, each in our own way.

In Their Hearts

Her People

Oh, Marta, my stoic pillar of strength, your people are here, your people are here!

"She is 96, you know," her daughter tells me, ever so proud of her German Mutter.[10] "Oh dear, oh dear, oh dear," we hear Marta chant in her thick accent every day when she tires of the chatter around her. Soon she will be asleep, head slumped over her walker. Marta needs her rest, you know. She has come so far in this life and she has worked hard, too. When her family comes to visit their Oma,[11] they are greeted by another resident on the Alzheimer's unit.

"Oh, Darlings, come right this way." says sweet southern Lily as she tries to pull them down the hall.

"No!" yells Marta. "These are my people! You go find your own people and leave my people alone!"

Marta smiles when she sees me each day. She thinks I am her distinguished doctor granddaughter of whom she is so proud. "Why have you come?" Marta inquires suspiciously of me.

It is ridiculous to say I am her chaplain, for 96-year-old women know more than I. "I have come to see you!" I reply.

---

[10]Mutter = German for "Mother".
[11]Oma = German for "Granny/Grandma".

A big toothless grin creeps across her face with a deep dark chuckle in her throat. "You are my people. Come and sit."

I do as ordered. "How are you, Marta?'

"I am good now that you are here." She pats my hand and her eyes beam with pride.

We sit in silence after that. Marta isn't one for long conversations anymore. One time I decided to test my broken German on her practiced ear.

"Tsk, tsk, your German is very bad. Do not talk now. You just sit here. Yes?"

"Yes, ma'am."

And so we sit here. Just Marta and me. We sit and we watch with 96-year-old eyes. We remember days gone by that will never return and we rest. Oh, how we rest.

Tonight Marta's hip and arm are broken. She is too old for surgery, but the pain is so great that she must be put under the knife tomorrow morning. Her daughter, intelligent and guarded, is surprised that I am at the hospital tonight. But it is my turn for night duty. I sit in the other rocking chair as Marta sleeps with morphine mixed in her bloodstream. The conversation is awkward, stilted, and then all of a sudden a story that has a life of its own slips from Marta's tired daughter's tongue.

"My mother is so strong, just so strong. I grew up in the northeast part of the United States. Because it was Hitler's time and because my parents were from Germany, the kids on my block called me a Nazi. I mean my parents were the most faithful Americans. You know, my mother is a devout Catholic, too. Two boys in particular always found a way to pick on me, to spit at and to hit me. One day I decided to defend myself against their attacks. I got my mother's broom and jammed the broomstick in their bicycle spokes. Their mothers came and told Marta she should punish me. My mother, bless her heart, said, 'Your boys are bad. My girl did right to take care of herself. You sue me if you do not agree.'"

I look at the sleeping Marta and I think of that strong woman who was in a strange new land when being German was considered evil in this country. Oh, Marta, don't die. Not yet. We need your strength. Don't leave us behind. We are so weak compared to you.

Later tonight every member of her family will be around Marta's bed. She will awake for a brief moment and they will say, "Marta, look! Your people are here! Your people are here!" And she will grin from ear to ear.

Oh, Marta, who are you to me? Why do I sit with you? Oh, Marta, my friend, I want to be one of your people too.

The next week I could foresee that Marta was going to die in the middle of the night. I arranged for a priest to come in the early morning hours. Marta died an hour after the priest gave her last rites. Her family had not asked, but I thought it was the least I could do.

Her daughter expressed deep appreciation for my last ministry.

Their Memorial Service

Memorial services are a traditional goodbye for the staff and families of Alzheimer residents who have lived on the unit for a long period of time and now have passed away. The tradition began long before I came and continued after my two years of work. At first I was told that the other residents on the unit shouldn't come because they wouldn't remember who died and they would upset the family. I wasn't so sure. In the flu season, during the winter months, residents die at a faster pace than during the rest of the year. The individual losses may not be remembered cognitively by the remaining residents, but I think their inner feelings know something sad has happened in and around their living quarters. I think those sad feelings need attention as do other parts of their lives. And so I asked the most recent family coming up to the unit for a memorial service if I could invite the residents. The family said they would like that.

I went to the day room and announced that we were having a memorial service down the hall. I said that someone who had lived on the floor had died. Would anyone like to come to the service? The woman who usually asks every five minutes what time it is asked me to tell her more about the person who had died. I said she was a wonderful woman who had spread her love onto all of us and that she would be missed. Seven residents decided to come to the service including the What-time-is-it?-woman. There were also about four family members and ten staff members present at the service.

The What-time-is-it?-woman sat down next to the daughter of the woman who had died. She turned to the daughter and said, "You were related, weren't you?"

"Yes, I am her daughter," was the polite response.

"I can tell you miss her very much. I can see it in your face."

"Yes," the daughter nodded.

"I'm sorry for your loss," said the What-time-is-it?-woman.

This conversation took place again and again during the memorial service. The other six residents participating in the service were not so dramatic. Neither did they act inappropriately. They and the What-time-is-it?-woman showed us that they understood their role as mourners. They sang the hymns in all seriousness and recited Psalm 23 with the rest of us and they listened to the eulogy. At the end they commented on what a nice service it was. The What-time-is-it?-woman told the grieving daughter one more time that she was sorry for her loss.

Later in private the daughter said it had meant so much to her to include the other residents. It made her feel that her mother's presence was most certainly there.

In Their Hearts

She Used To Sing

She used to sing and her eyes would twinkle at me. She was a minister's wife, you know. Knew every hymn in the book, and played the piano all those years. The hymns grounded her, made her sing and smile like sunshine.

Now she sits and looks at a piece of lint caught on the end of her thumb. She falls asleep during the devotional time, a time she used to love. Other times she sees something in the air that the rest of us cannot see.

One day I was telling a story and just at the right moment she blurted out, "Isn't that just like a man?" I suppose if anyone else had said it, it wouldn't have been funny, but this was a prim and proper preacher's wife who had raised her children to be stoic, clean and humble. When she said that, I broke into a gut-wrenching laugh. She had topped this storyteller, made the punch line better than my own. She laughed too.

Now she doesn't laugh or sing for herself or for me or for her family. And I wonder where she has gone. Will she sing again one last time or is she saving it up for the day she and Jesus kiss in heaven?

I have to admit I miss that sweet angelic melody that flowed like milk and honey each week. She knew how to sing the descant harmony, her voice so young and beautiful in contrast to her aging shell.

Now I sit by her bedside and sing to her in my own simple way not meant for any ear but hers. I hope it helps her in this journey from life to death, though I may never know if she ever heard me.

She used to sing and in my heart she always will. Oh please, oh please, sing to me.

The Son
(of She Used to Sing)

He cried the day his mama died, wiped the tears with his sleeve, and moved on from that place in time. He had things to do, a service to plan, family to call. I watched, helpless to do anything, her body between us no longer singing.

At the memorial service he kept busy and talked a lot. Then something bigger than himself broke him in two with big gut-wrenching sobs and my heart broke for him. What's a minister to do?

I wonder where mommies go when their babies cry, when strong arms disappear from our reality. Who rocks the children then?

He is big physically and professionally, but size doesn't matter when mommies go away. Mommies will always be mommies and sons will always be sons.

One day I will leave my own son and I won't be there to hold him anymore. I wonder where I will go until we meet again. Will I pace anxiously on streets of gold or shoot hoops in the sky? Will I argue with Jesus for a century or bake blackberry pie?

He cried the day his mother died and she wasn't there to hold him anymore. Gone is her voice, her touch, her smile, her eyes that knew all things. When mamas die and go to the sky, they leave behind precious brokenhearted children who can't let go, because a mama will always be a mama and a son will always be a son.

I don't know why we are made like this. Who thought of such a creation? But, there is no turning back now. We are already here, mothers and sons everywhere.

I, the minister, will watch and know pain will always be pain, death will always be death, and love will always be love between a mother and a son.

Monster Woman

She is dying. There is no turning back. I sit beside her bed and whisper sweet nothings. Sitting next to her does not soothe the pain of losing her. I don't even know why I feel anything--why I would miss this woman who is so frightening, so much like the monsters in my nightmares.

She used to scream out in the devotional time when she saw bizarre images inside her head. She would yell at me to get rid of the spiders or whatever else ailed her. "GET THEM! AAAAHHHHHH! GET THEM OFF OF ME!" she would cry out, so distressed by the creatures only she could see.

Reluctantly I would swat at her ghosts and goblins, angry that I couldn't continue my story or homily. The woman was a disruption. She messed up the little bit of order I was so proud to bring to the Alzheimer's unit.

I was informed by different members of the staff that years ago she loved church. Her chart confirmed their words about her history. For a long time I didn't want to feel anything for her, even though there was evidence there was more to her than the screaming. "This lady is just too crazy for me," I thought to myself as my heart stomped around in my chest angrily.

But still she screeched during our sacred time. "COME HERE! I SAID, 'COME HERE!'" Her voice is more frightening than that of any creature I can make up in my mind. "COME HERE! GET OVER HERE NOW!" She didn't stop until she had her withered hand vise-gripped around my wrist. I was always reminded of the Wicked Witch from the "Wizard of Oz" as she said to Dorothy, "Come here, my little pretty."

Amazingly, after ten minutes into the devotional time each week the monsters and creepy-crawly things would quit haunting her. She was at peace for a few short minutes. When our worship time was over she was back to yelling and snatching at me when I walked too close to her wheelchair.

The monsters in her head turned her into a monster in reality. All day long they taunted and teased and danced a jig in her brain, the brain that has been labeled by modern doctors, "Dementia! Right here!"

Some days between the obnoxious screaming, a tiny little-girl voice would take a tumble out of her mouth and tug at my heart when she would give up fighting her lizards and bees. "I'm scared. Please hold my hand. Oh, please stay here with me." I would tiptoe next to her and she would whisper, "It's so scary being me. Can you help me? Can you help me, please?"

I would pull up a chair and brush the hair off of her face with my timid fingers, still afraid she would tear into me. But she wouldn't yell or scream. She would take my hand and say, "Please don't ever leave me here alone with them. Please make them go away!"

Deep down inside of me a trap door would pry itself open and see her with empathy. Oh, Molly, I will never leave you. I am here beside you. I am so sorry for your chamber of horrors that makes you act like one of its demons. Why do you have to die? No one else is as good at interrupting me as you with your tough outside and soft center. I won't leave you. I won't leave you. I will sit and sing and pray as you draw your last breaths. "Monsters, leave my friend alone! Jesus, hold Molly safe in your arms! Oh, Molly, I don't want you to go. Please stay with me. Who else will understand my own monsters in my own head? You sat at the edge of my own reality. You and your pictures helped me believe I'm not a bad person for having ghosts and goblins haunt me. You see, Molly, you framed me. You made it safer to be me. I will miss you terribly. Goodbye, my Molly. I'm glad you are finally free of your body. I'm glad your misery is over. Fly away and dance with Jesus every day for eternity. Goodbye."

When Too Many Die

Another person is dead and I don't want to go back to the unit. Of course they will all die eventually. We all will. This does not protect me from the loss of so many. Sometimes it just gets to me and I don't want to go back today or tomorrow. What am I supposed to do? I know I will complain to Woody and stomp about more than usual. I will stand next to the stream on this beautiful property and feel the gentle breeze on my skin. I will ask Jesus if he still knows me. Jesus will whisper in my ear and I will resign myself to my humanity. No matter what, I don't have the power to bring them back except on these pages that I write and in my personal memories. I don't think they would really want to come back to the disease that robbed them of their memory and that separated them from a lot of the human community.

Even though so many have died, I will never let go of them completely. When so many have died, I just can't accept it entirely. If I felt the sadness all at one time, my heart would slide right out of my chest. If I sat down and counted all those I have buried, I wouldn't want to stand up again. Instead, I think of them still alive, singing, dancing, fighting, joking, complaining, winking, and all those other things they do. I remember them with pride, for they did their best against, and with, the dementia. They did more than suffer. They survived and lived out their days in their own special ways. I hope they know how much I appreciate that they let me go with them on part of the journey. I hope they know they made me a better chaplain. I hope they know they touched me.

Excuse Me, I'm So Sorry

I'm crying tonight because I don't want to see her in pain anymore. I've known Nettie Mae for nineteen months. In a care plan meeting I attended last year Nettie Mae was described as having low self-esteem because when she comes into a room she says to all the people she passes "Excuse me, I'm so sorry." I'm not convinced it is an esteem issue. I remember being told as a child that I had to have something called manners. I assume Nettie Mae was told the same thing.

Last year during Holy Week, Nettie Mae and I sang every Christmas song we could remember. We giggled and laughed out loud for ourselves because we remembered so many words we thought we had forgotten. When we were all sung out, I said, "I just love it here with you and the others. I can have Good Friday and Christmas all in the same day!"

"Isn't it great!" Nettie Mae agreed.

"Well, I hate to say this, Miss Nettie Mae, but I've got to go." I mentioned reluctantly.

"Oh, Darling," she said to me, "please come back and see me."

"I will," I promised.

Nettie Mae has come to more religious events than anyone else on the unit.

"I'm Baptist, you know," she reports to me every week. "Are you Baptist too?" she asks innocently because she cannot remember my reply from the last time she asked me.

"Yes, Nettie Mae, I'm Baptist too."

"Well, then, we can be Baptist together!" she says with a satisfied look upon her gentle face.

I don't know if she has Parkinson's or Tourette's or a reaction to one of her medications. She has to pat with her hands constantly. Nettie Mae pats her chest, pats her head, pats her other hand, pats her hip, and pats her knees when she sits down. The patting irritates the other residents.

"Stop that!" they yell. "Stop hitting yourself!"

Nettie Mae says, "Oh, excuse me, I'm so sorry."

I take her by the hand and sit her next to me. "Here, Nettie Mae, sit here, you can pat yourself all you want next to me."

She beams as she says, "Thank you, Darling. This is one of the reasons I love you. You let me be me."

"Oh, Nettie Mae, you are such a sweetheart," I can't help but gush.

"You think so? You really think so? Me, a sweetheart? Can that be possible?" She is caught by surprise every time. I often think about when humility was a good thing in this society--a long time ago.

"Oh, Nettie Mae, you will always be a sweetheart in my eyes," I admit, just as I do every time I see her.

"Then it must be so." She giggles as she looks at me.

My weekly routine looks like this: List of things to do in my head - #1 Go get Nettie Mae for our devotional / church time. #2 Now, we can start because Nettie Mae is here.

"Is church about to start? Don't start without me.?" She pleads when she sees me.

"Come right this way, Miss Nettie Mae, and we'll go to church together," I say, slowing down my pace to match hers.

"Why, thank you, Darling. Just lead the way. I'm right behind you," says Nettie Mae every week, so very happy for church to get started again.

Two weeks ago she broke her hip and had surgery. This weekend she had a stroke and now her body is married to the bed. I look at her hopelessly.

"Oh, Nettie Mae! Oh, Nettie Mae!"

Her speech is slurred, "Yep, it's me, Darling. It hurts, Darling, it hurts all over. I'm so glad you came. I'm just so glad you came."

I feel tears rolling down my cheeks. "Oh, Nettie Mae, it is so hard to see you like this."

"Tell me about it, Darling. I'm the one like this!" retorts Nettie Mae sarcastically.

I giggle, "You are so witty even when you are hurting."

"I can't help it, Darling. I just wish it wasn't so hard. It's just so hard."

"Should we pray to Jesus, Nettie Mae?" I ask my Baptist comrade.

"Yes, we should, Darling. I love Jesus so and I love you. I've loved you a long time now, Darling. Don't you forget that."

And then there is silence. Squirrels scurry in the trees outside Nettie Mae's window. They are on another planet from Nettie Mae and me. I run my hands through her sweaty hair as I quit fighting the tears.

"Give me your hand!" demands Nettie Mae in a most un-lady-like way. I put my hand in her still-useful left hand, for the hand on the right is frozen with the stiffness of the stroke. "Now you listen to me!" she begins. "I love you so much, Darling! Do you hear me, Darling? I love you so much. Answer me! Do you hear me?"

"I hear you," I barely breathe.

"Good, because it is important that you know that. I need you to know I love you before I can't tell you anymore."

Oh, Nettie Mae, I love you too. I love you too!

Chapter Five - Parting

Parting

My ministry on my first Special Care Alzheimer's Unit came to an abrupt end after two years when funding didn't come through. Six months later more money would arrive. Although my ministry has now picked up on other Alzheimer's units, I have not returned to the unit that birthed these stories. Some of the residents I knew before have moved to my new units. This is special to me but I left many people behind. I cried many tears in my last weeks on my first Alzheimer's unit. This book is in honor and memory of all the people I met on that unit. It is my way of remembering everyone. This book ends with a poem written by Jim Fowler. He writes that I, too, will be remembered. I found his poem a great comfort as my heart broke over leaving these beloved Alzheimer's residents.

When I was twenty-one a childhood friend died in a car crash. A year after her death I found I had a choice to make about the eternal hole in my heart. I could let it dominate my life by letting my heart grow smaller as I forever raged at God. Or I could let my heart grow larger to include the new people in my life. I chose the latter. Seventeen years later I still miss my childhood friend, but I also have more loving to do before I leave this earth. In this same manner I will forever miss the individuals in these stories, but I will move on and love more Alzheimer's residents on more units.

Do You Know My Name? – Part II

Two years after our first meeting Julia Norman was still telling me her name even though she recognized my face and she understood I was no longer new. I suppose she was just making sure I remembered her. Sometimes I am like that with God. I pray, "This is Mary Margaret. Do you remember me?" Perhaps it is I who forgets God and Julia and a lot of other important folk. But I still ask if God remembers me.

In the quiet of the day room after Julia Norman had introduced herself once again, she leaned toward me and said, "You know, you and I are a lot alike."

"We are?" I forgot to sound calm. She still knew how to catch me off guard, for of course Julia Norman, N-o-r-m-a-n was still in charge of the conversation.

"Yes," she continued as she caught my eye to make sure I was listening. "You know Mama could always count on me. When folks asked something of her and she couldn't do it because of her health, she would say, 'Julia can do it!' And I'd do it too. You see, my dear, once someone has bragged on you and they believe in you, you might as well follow through." Julia Norman stopped for a moment to let my young brain catch up to her wisdom before she continued with, "I can tell someone has bragged on you, because I see you work so hard in this place. So I was figuring that you must be following through. Tell me I'm not right."

"It's true," I confessed in my astonishment that she had given me the biggest compliment a Norman could give, for to be compared to a Norman is to be counted in with a tribe of right-smart hard-working folks.

Julia Norman flashed a rare smile and said with a pat on my back, "Well, good for you. I'm sorry I can't stay. I've got things to do. We Normans are busy, busy folks, you know. Keep up the good work, Darlin', and I'll see ya' next time. Love ya'. And by the way, you need to visit me more often." And with the wave of her hand she was gone to inspect things, here and there, up and down the hall.

"Do you know my name? Do you know me? Julia Norman. N-o-r-m-a-n."

The Newest Resident

She is so beautiful and full of life that I never think of her as old. She is somewhere between the beginning and the middle of the long journey called Alzheimer's disease. I can see in her eyes and in her comments that she is afraid of becoming like the others. In the meantime she has taken the attitude that she will have all the fun she can as long as she can. She travels around the building playing Bingo and baking cookies and doing other fun things. In between activities she reads delightful books she wants to pass on to me. "Oh, you will like this one. It is so wonderful and so funny!" On Saturdays she and her daughter go shopping for the cutest clothes that I get to see the next week. "Isn't this just the most darling blouse? We just bought it at Rich's. And it was on sale, too!" she tells me with pride. I find her in her room some days. It is as immaculate and lovely as her dress. It reminds me of my grandmother's parlor with the antiques and old portraits on the wall. Her room is the antithesis of any institution. It is so welcoming that both staff and residents want to visit.

The first time she heard me tell a story she fell in love with my verbal abilities. She clapped loudly and said, "More, more! We must have more!" That is the day I became her trusted buddy. She began placing her hand on my arm and saying, "You wouldn't believe what I have seen today. My lord, you would think some of these folks would have more sense. Bless their hearts. They can't help it. That one hit that other one over there and that one took off all his clothes. Sometimes it's a regular zoo up here. Are you going to tell any stories today? Please say you will."

Little by little I watch her memory trickle away like a leaky faucet. She notices it, too. She says, "It worries me, just worries me so. I'm just not as sharp as I used to be. I feel so stupid sometimes." It is difficult to witness her decline. I don't mind saying I don't think it is fair that she is robbed of her own brain. Doesn't God care? How can such an elegant creature be dismantled little by little? I wonder where God is in times like these? Then I see God in her baby blue eyes pleading with me to visit just a little bit longer so she can forget for another moment what is happening to her.

It bothers me that I am leaving next month. I don't have the heart to tell her. She will be angry with me just as she is every time I miss story hour or get called away from one of our private visits. How can I leave someone who needs me? I don't know how I can do it. I just don't know how I can do it.

Hey, Preach! - Part II

He no longer speaks of his small town as he did when I first met him. He barely says a word. But he chuckles with a twinkle in his eye when he sees me coming his way. I figure I am still the "Preach" in his small hometown as he used to call me. But who is to know for sure?

In a month my time as chaplain will be up. After two years on this particular Alzheimer's unit, I will have to leave my beloved Tommy. I suppose a new "Preach" will take my place. I hope the new "Preach" knows he or she is in Tommy's small town, not in the big city as it appears to you and me. And I hope the new "Preach" knows some outlandish good ol' southern stories for Tommy's sake. Tommy needs to laugh so hard that tears roll down his cheeks. He also needs to wink at some secret every day.

What will I do without Tommy's hometown to visit? What will I do without his delightful view of reality? Sometimes I wonder who helps whom more. Can we be sliced down the middle like that? Perhaps we are who we are because of each other. Goodbye, Tommy's hometown. I enjoyed living in you for an hour or two each day. God, please take care of Tommy--if not for you, then for Tommy and me.

(Tommy died unexpectedly two weeks before I left the unit.)

If I Get Alzheimer's

If I get Alzheimer's, please send me to a place with Siamese kittens and newborn babies. I also want to see women's basketball and soccer on the TV. Don't make me come to sing-alongs or sit me next to someone who irritates me. I want intelligent conversations on feminist spirituality. I don't mind making a cupcake or two with chocolate icing and m&m candy. I need you to know I like resting in a big ol' comfy rocking chair in the evening right after a meal of fresh boiled shrimp and buttery cornbread. I'll listen to the bobwhites sing about their territory and the crickets chirp to set my spirit free. I need field trips to some whitewater rivers like the Chattooga, Section-III. Let me dip my hand in the water to feel it lapping at my wrinkled skin. I'll listen to the pines whispering their pride that I have had a wonderful life journey.

Don't think me crazy when I lift my hands to the sky and answer the wind by howling over the loss of my precious memories. Please don't tell me not to cry when I can't find my mommy and daddy in the wee morning hours when the monsters chase me awake again. I'm not always happy now and I don't expect to change my pensive personality for some young fool who thinks he or she knows better for me. If you ask if I've been saved or born again, I just might kick you in the shin for being status quo and for asking me something I already know.

Tell me stories of the good ol' days when Melissa Etheridge ruled rock & roll. Let me tell you who I am and where I've been. I don't care if I help you with your research paper on dementia. I just want someone to get to know me. Do you know I've been loved by the best of them in my lifetime? Do you care?

So what that I've earned two Masters degrees? For life ain't nothing without witty comebacks and homemade butter pecan ice cream.

If I get Alzheimer's, don't think you already know me because I have this disease. I am more than my lost memory. I am me, and you must spend time with me to get to know me. Whether or not your budget allows it, I want your minutes and your heart, for if you get Alzheimer's, I wouldn't expect any less from me.

Ripping the Quilt

It's like ripping a quilt patch by patch. That's what it is like to leave them. One of the certified nursing assistants says to me, "When is your last day?" I stare at her in shock. Last day? What is that? We are only beginning to understand each other. How can I leave? What is this thing called money that decides our fate? Who makes such decisions? Do we even need chaplains? No matter the reason, I leave in three weeks. We are forever knitting together and forever pulling apart. Rip. Rip. Someone, stop this painful process! Take me to a time when I never knew them. This is too much for my heart. I don't want to go. We are torn scraps of quilt thrown to the wind. Where we will land I just don't know.

Goodbye, Julia Norman. I won't forget your name. Goodbye, Sweet Southern Lily and the "I Love You" woman who walks me up and down the hall. Goodbye, Rose, who sneaks candy. Goodbye, George, who never tells why he follows me. Goodbye, "What-Time-Is-It?"-woman. Others will answer your questions and bring you peanut butter crackers. Goodbye, Deborah, who prayed for our activity therapist, Melanie. Goodbye, Mr. Jackson. This time we will not go together. Goodbye, new folks I was just getting to know. I am sorry I couldn't get to know you better.

Goodbye, Jesus, who lives with them and is in them, too. I have to go now. I will write about you and I will remember you and I will carry your spirit with me forever.

Love,
MM

This Is (To) Mary Margaret Yearwood
By Jim Fowler

Mary Margaret, Mary Margaret,
in your stories and your poems
you gradually came out
in moments,
relations, loves, generously lavished
on those whose acceptance
and gratitude are failing but unfeigned,
finite but courageous,
fragmented yet curiously whole.

Leavings bring such painful sorrows.
So often you have been left--gradually, gradually,
and then, finally--
by those on whom you've poured out love
in song, in story, in touch, in prayer,
in faithful attendance to their souls.
And now you leave.

In those places of the heart
where soul still lurks,
they will remember.
In tactile hunger for hands that caress and care,
they will remember.

In ringing ears longing for the lilt of music,
they will remember.

At heaven's gate
where all the leaves
of lost memories are restored,
they WILL remember
all the loving fragments, melodies, touches,
prayers and tales by which you loved them.
Angels will sing, dance and shout,
sensing your love in these loved ones' joys.

God bless you for your love and care
and accompany you in your continued ministry
of writing, song, prayer, and care.

*Jim Fowler is a professor at Emory University
and an author of numerous books.*

ISBN 155395431-9

9 781553 954316